Palgrave Studies in Affect Theory and Literary Criticism

Series Editors
Joel Faflak
Western University
London, Canada

Richard C. Sha
Literature Department
American University
Washington, USA

The recent surge of interest in affect and emotion has productively crossed disciplinary boundaries within and between the humanities, social sciences, and sciences, but has not often addressed questions of literature and literary criticism as such. The first of its kind, Palgrave Studies in Affect Theory and Literary Criticism seeks theoretically informed scholarship that examines the foundations and practice of literary criticism in relation to affect theory. This series aims to stage contemporary debates in the field, addressing topics such as: the role of affective experience in literary composition and reception, particularly in non-Western literatures; examinations of historical and conceptual relations between major and minor philosophies of emotion and literary experience; and studies of race, class, gender, sexuality, age, and disability that use affect theory as a primary critical tool.

Louis Charland †, Western University, Canada
Patrick Colm Hogan, University of Connecticut, USA
Holly Crocker, University of South Carolina, USA
David James, University of Birmingham, UK
Julia Lupton, University of California Irvine, USA
Kate Singer, Mount Holyoke College, USA
Jane Thrailkill, University of North Carolina at Chapel Hill, USA
Donald Wehrs, Auburn University, USA

Matthew Phillips

Disorder, Affect, and Modernist Literature

Empathy After Entropy

Matthew Phillips
University of North Carolina at Greensboro
Greensboro, NC, USA

ISSN 2634-6311　　　　　　ISSN 2634-632X　(electronic)
Palgrave Studies in Affect Theory and Literary Criticism
ISBN 978-3-031-92462-0　　ISBN 978-3-031-92463-7　(eBook)
https://doi.org/10.1007/978-3-031-92463-7

© The Editor(s) (if applicable) and The Author(s), under exclusive license to Springer Nature Switzerland AG 2025

This work is subject to copyright. All rights are solely and exclusively licensed by the Publisher, whether the whole or part of the material is concerned, specifically the rights of translation, reprinting, reuse of illustrations, recitation, broadcasting, reproduction on microfilms or in any other physical way, and transmission or information storage and retrieval, electronic adaptation, computer software, or by similar or dissimilar methodology now known or hereafter developed.
The use of general descriptive names, registered names, trademarks, service marks, etc. in this publication does not imply, even in the absence of a specific statement, that such names are exempt from the relevant protective laws and regulations and therefore free for general use.
The publisher, the authors and the editors are safe to assume that the advice and information in this book are believed to be true and accurate at the date of publication. Neither the publisher nor the authors or the editors give a warranty, expressed or implied, with respect to the material contained herein or for any errors or omissions that may have been made. The publisher remains neutral with regard to jurisdictional claims in published maps and institutional affiliations.

This Palgrave Macmillan imprint is published by the registered company Springer Nature Switzerland AG.
The registered company address is: Gewerbestrasse 11, 6330 Cham, Switzerland

If disposing of this product, please recycle the paper.

Contents

1 Introduction — 1

2 Writing as Rescue in Stephen Crane's "The Open Boat" — 23

3 Entropic Affect in Jean Toomer's "Withered Skin of Berries" — 35

4 Necessary Entropy in Virginia Woolf's *To the Lighthouse* — 49

5 Darkening Empathy in Eugene O'Neill's *Long Day's Journey into Night* — 63

Index — 77

CHAPTER 1

Introduction

Abstract In this introduction, I show that Silvan Tomkins's affect system is an effective critical apparatus for evaluating literary modernism's unique handling of character. Well acquainted with the physical sciences, Tomkins instills foundational thermodynamic concepts into his theories, revealing that affect behaves entropically. Tomkins encourages us to envision the conscious self as consonant not only with the coterminous internal subsystems with which the self overlaps and intermingles, but also with the external systems that house the self. Such a model allows for fresh examinations of modernism's situation and formation of character within entropic settings. Modernism's sharp focus on the individual, in turn, underscores that meaning is made, not in isolation, but by virtue of connections formed within a network of systems. The individual, therefore, becomes a case study for experiences that are widely applicable. Affect theory provides the lexicon for these robust new analyses of character within the intricate networks exemplified in modernist literature.

Keywords Accumulation • Affect • Disorder • Entropy • Equilibrium • Heat death • Modernism • Shame • Thermodynamics • Tomkins, Silvan

This book offers analyses of a selection of texts both representative of and meaningfully adjacent to literary modernism. The readings that follow are principally based on the pervasive manifestations of entropy in both the spirit and the writing of the period augmented by the substantiation of a significant tie between those manifestations and the affect system popularized by Silvan Tomkins. The affect system is an effective critical apparatus—one that considers both the scientific and the emotional—for evaluating modernism's unique handling of character within entropic contexts. Best known for his lifelong exploration of affect, Tomkins was well-acquainted with the physical sciences, not least thermodynamics, and he instilled its key concepts into his theories. Read this way, Tomkins reveals that affect behaves entropically. Entropy and affect continuously increase within a system until that system reaches an equilibrium. In entropy's case, equilibrium results in a thermal homogeneity called heat death. When an individual undergoes an accumulation of affect, on the other hand, equilibrium serves to dissolve intrapersonal and interpersonal obstructions theretofore unyielding. On the textual level, Tomkins's model also permits a richer exploration of what George Lakoff and Mark Johnson term a "container metaphor," our tendency to "impose boundaries" where none naturally exist; to conceptualize planets, people, what have you, as closed systems, "containers with an inside and an outside" (29). Tomkins's body-as-system model encourages us to envision the conscious self as not only consonant with the multitude of coterminous internal subsystems with which the self overlaps and intermingles (cardiovascular, digestive), but also with the external systems that house the self (a society, a planet). This model of the person as "a bio-psycho-social entity at the intersect of both more complex higher social systems and lower biological systems" allows for fresh examinations of modernism's situation and formation of literary character within numerous entropic settings ("Quest" 308). Modernism's sharp focus on the individual, in turn, highlights that it is indeed by virtue of the connections retained as part of a network of systems that one finds and makes meaning. We therefore recognize the individual as a case study for experiences that are, in fact, widely applicable. Tomkins provides us with a lexicon for such robust new analyses of character within any number of intricate networks exemplified in modernist literature.

Furthermore, by virtue of an "algorithmic" tracing of the "dynamic and changeable" in Tomkins, my aim is to provide a study that "amplifies the important and undertheorized middle ranges of affective agency" championed by Adam J. Frank and Elizabeth A. Wilson (98–99). Censuring theories that "unilaterally favor flux over stasis or process over organization," Frank and Wilson advance that in place of "arguing for static personality structures" or "for infinitely multiplying iterations affective events, Tomkins gives us a model of theory building as construction, breakdown, renewal, and reassembly within a known number of parameters" (98). "Known number of parameters" is operative here if we consider heat death. Certainly, entropy engenders "breakdown, renewal, and reassembly"—but there is an endgame. Hence, witnessing affect acting entropically reveals "the heart of Tomkins's account of affect theory": the "oscillation between the importance of skilled defenses against negative affects, on one hand, and the breakdown of those defenses, on the other."

I also align with Rita Felski and Toril Moi, whose recent work exonerates character analysis and updates how we think about character identification. All these concepts—entropy, affect, character identification—are functionally bound by a propensity toward dissolution. Consider this excerpt from Felski: "Affinities experienced while reading a book or watching a film can cut across divisions of gender, race, sexuality, class, or even, in certain genres, species. It is a matter not just of finding oneself but of leaving oneself" (81). In this example, character identification makes possible the breach of any number of interpersonal "divisions." The Janus-faced act of "finding" and "leaving oneself" suggests an overall increase of freedom, in the sense that Tomkins uses the word. One's freedom increases relative to one's "wants" alongside one's "capacities to satisfy them"; "Restriction" of either means a decrease in freedom (Tomkins, *Shame* 36).[1] Constraint results in shame, the state of "being suspended between what [one] wants and what [one] can have" (Frank and Wilson 67). That which incites the wearing away of impediments (entropy, affect, identification), that which results in an increase of freedom, denotes a net positive. Familiarity with these processes advances our construal of the human connections and shared experiences mirrored in modernist literature.

Modernism and Entropy

Accounts of literary modernism have been known to echo descriptions of ruins—disassembled fragments of some long-defunct edifice, bits and pieces of an epoch itself affectively bankrupt. One would be forgiven for

---

[1] Hereafter cited *Shame*.

asking whether modernism bemoaned or exalted disorder. Modernist studies to date has generally concentrated on demolition, with less consideration given to how entropic conditions alter human affect and emotion in constructive ways. Julie Taylor theorizes that if the period's "affective dimensions have historically been under-researched, perhaps this is because scholars have tended to emphasize modernists' aesthetic preferences for irony and detachment over embodied sentiment" (2). More recently, David James, spotting a corresponding sea change in new modernist studies, says the "solidity of modernism's own cultural, formal, and institutional coherence is now being dissolved under pressures of reform that not only leave it unanchored from any single 'movement' but also liberate its aesthetic practices from the impersonal language of rupture that has seemed inimical to a more expansive range of affective readings" (130). Despite its connotations of distance and dispassion, fresh attention to the sincere interpretations of inner life scattered throughout modernism threatens its icy exterior in stirring ways. In company with affect, the entropic modernist experience of alienation, disorder, and system deterioration is not merely negative, but productive in facilitating new structures of feeling and social adhesion.

This is not to say, given modernism's entropic temperament, that the laws of thermodynamics don't equally provide means for warmer evaluation. As Mark Morrison attests, the "shifting modes of scientific understanding that classical thermodynamics straddled have allowed modernist studies to be particularly in tune with the ideologies and formal reach of thermodynamics in modernist culture" (43). One might summarize thermodynamics as a concern with heat (temperature-motivated energy) and its capacity to travel between bodies of matter called systems. The accumulation of waste energy ensuant to heat exchange is known as entropy. What we understand today of entropy and thermodynamics results from theories that surfaced in the decades leading up to the fin de siècle. Researchers across Europe broke ground in the field of classical thermodynamics in the early to mid-nineteenth century. In time they observed that although "energy was not destroyed as it was converted into the work of a mechanical engine, some of it was always lost, often through friction, as wasted heat. In 1850, the German physicist Rudolf Clausius gave this dissipation, this increasing lack of availability of energy for work, a name: entropy" (Morrison 43). Priorities consequently shifted away from thermodynamics' first law (energy can change form but cannot be created nor destroyed) to its second (heat travels one way only, from warmer to cooler sources), a concomitant intellectual turn in tow (Morrison 41). The discovery that systems tend towards decline under the accumulation of wasted energy, that usable energy within a system is finite, reverberated beyond the sciences into other arenas.

Critics continue to add to the hardy exploration entropy enjoys: Matthew Wraith gives it a human face, noting that shivering is the "ultimate form of entropic vibration": "We shiver to preserve ourselves, to try to maintain our warm-blooded homeostasis. But in doing so, we merely hasten out own entropic decay" (100). Woolf's most entropic novel, *To the Lighthouse*, draws plenty of attention from modernists. Justin Sausman remarks that the tension Woolf creates between "vibration and stillness emphasizes the gap between life and fiction" (45). Robert Milder labels entropy in *Lighthouse* an "antagonist," the "force that renders human beings insufficient" (145). For Martin Meisel, who adorns the book with a "'luminous halo,'" disorder is "redeemed" in the "risk-taking novel in which Woolf the writer found her freedom" (28). I value especially this optimistic reading from Graham Fraser:

> The Ramsay's summerhouse is—architecturally, domestically, metaphorically—very much a Victorian, nineteenth-century home. Reading its fall into ruin as an architectural metaphor for the abandonment of an untenable, nineteenth-century aesthetic at the dawn of the Modernist era opens the way to read its ruin as a case study in renovation—a modernist 'making it new'—that, paradoxically, requires the old to fall into disrepair. (119)

Marcus Nicholls has also been somewhat of an entropy apologist as of late. In coining "interpretive entropy" and "reception decay," Nicholls argues these phenomena offer readers "interpretive gaps within which subjective intertexts might burrow, perforating the integrity of the text in order to form new versions" (327). I concur with this appeal to give entropy a second life in three dimensions, to "recycle the concept of decay more significantly" (Nicholls 327). Fraser, too, emphasizes that entropy represents not a state, but a process: "Woolf depicts the collapse of the house not as a fixed or final state but as a trajectory of decay that both reveals the work of time in its structural transformation and resonates with the other instances of artistic creation that bracket it in the first and third parts of the novel. Art in *To the Lighthouse* is less about the art work than art working" (128). Work is undeniably of special importance in modernism. Writers exhausted themselves mentally, physically, emotionally; breakdowns were common. If refocusing the dominant scientific worldview acutely on entropy demanded "negotiations between aesthetic and scientific practices," then a "new language for modernity" was also needed; a language of "energy, of lines of force" (Bell 115).

I have argued elsewhere in a similar tenor about Jean Toomer's masterpiece, *Cane*. Published in 1923, Toomer's best-known book is a hybrid tour de force that captures in prose and poetry his firsthand account of a vanishing spiritual energy within the African American population of the South. His "anxiety about the entropic forces primed to lay waste to the southern, African American folk-spirit is central to our understanding of *Cane*; however, Toomer sees promise for racial equilibrium in the resulting heat-death" (Phillips 204). My concession is this: if *Cane* "presents us with potential, the text itself does not leave us with clear examples of what possibilities such potential provides" (Phillips 223). What remains clear is that the racial equilibrium explored in *Cane* was "not only political; it was personal" (Phillips 223). Toomer's modernist mainstay suffers no emotive shortage. He uses *Cane* not only to foreground the disordered and dichotomous worlds he navigates, but also to bridge the gap between those worlds. Toomer's use of entropic environments and situations demonstrates entropy's capacity to, as Nicholls might say, "perforat[e] the integrity of [societies disgraced by discrimination] in order to form new versions" (327). If *Cane* defies traditional literary form, it is because Toomer "would far rather form a man than form a book" (19). As we shall see in Chap. 2, Toomer uses similar strategies in his contemporaneous short story "Withered Skin of Berries" (1922).

Prior to modernism per se, the publishing world was already working to "Make It New." Cara Murray observes how the large-scale shift away from the first law's primacy affected the nascent *Dictionary of National Biography*, offering insight into the human cost of entropy at its inception. "Mired in entropy," the *DNB*'s "unfettered accumulation of materials, the disorganized state of the archives, underdeveloped methods for sorting facts" was an unlikely source of reassurance for its first editor, Leslie Stephen (Murray 88–89). It was not so much the content of the *DNB* as "the mood of its makers" that was affected: "For all of Stephen's moaning about the 'powers of chaos and darkness,' he embraced the entropic mood" (Murray 89). On the contrary, "It was precisely his entropy-centric attitude that enabled him to resist entropy and, by so doing, to usher the *DNB* into the information age." Instead of hastening its downfall, Stephen's acceptance of entropy allowed him to futureproof the *DNB*. In a noteworthy historical parallel, the acquiescence to disorder across Stephen's domain offers a reflection of entropy's coincident, far-reaching acceptance in microcosm:

> [T]he dominant form of biography prior to entropy's rule, self-help, depended upon a belief in limitless energy…. [S]elf-help was predicated on the idea that men improved machines and thereby improved themselves, ad infinitum. Self-help therefore promoted a utopic worldview in which man and machine never stopped improving. But the infinitely available energy that fueled this genre dried up with the popularization of entropy, and in the decades following Clausius's findings, biographies of ambitious individuals with ceaseless energy made less sense. (Murray 88–89)

In the ensuing decades, amidst a wartime turn from Hegelian optimism to the toil of existentialism, luminaries of the literary world also underscored energy's expenditure. Ian F. A. Bell argues that modernism's "artisanal emphasis" and penchant for the technical aspects of poetry is a symptom of the same intellectual changes that influenced so many others around the century's turn (115). In 1915's "The Love Song of J. Alfred Prufrock," T. S. Eliot's patent "self-consciousness thrusts the technique of the simile upon us [so] emphasizing the *work* of literary procedure" (Bell 114–15). It wasn't just poets: "Identification, emotional responses, sympathy, and moralism must go," Moi writes, "for they serve only to cloud the critics gaze …. [I]t's not just character criticism but realism itself that must go" (Moi 43). As if to mirror the entropic dissolution of all things, modernists and their critics dismantle language, feeling, reality. Privilege not the poet or the poem; only tradition, work. These ways of thinking, Moi argues, "still police the boundaries of our discipline" (47): "Literary studies today, then, are dominated by a two-headed troll: formalism and theory. Both draw on and incorporate the pro-modernist agenda that inspired the first generation of professional academic critics" (48). This "agenda" has led to a rift between serious scholarship and character analysis. But I will show that, in rejecting reality, the modernists clasped hands with the realest of realisms when they subsumed the entropic into their work.

Entropy and Affect

On the face of it, affect and entropy make bizarre bedfellows. However, they share numerous traits. Neither substance nor observable force, entropy is the measurement of a system's accumulation of waste energy over time. Entropy results in equilibrium, the state in which all matter in a system is at the same temperature. Megan Watkins observes how affect is similarly "retained" across events, its accrual apt to "shape subjectivities" (269): affect is "not viewed as simply transient in quality. These states of being are not only momentary. Through the iteration of similar experiences … they accumulate in the form of what could be considered dispositions that predispose one to act and react in particular ways" (278). Just as entropy builds unseen, "affect also operates independently, accumulating as *bodily* memory that … may evade consciousness altogether" (279). As time progresses and experiences gather, both affect and entropy compile, altering how systems behave. These two accumulative phenomena—one internal, subjective; the other external, objective—do not operate exclusively; taken together, both processes provide richer appreciation of what motivates the behavior of a system and its inhabitants.

As stated above, Tomkins is best known for his lifelong exploration of the affect system: the "primary motivational system in human beings" (*Shame* 34). Tomkins was exposed to the emerging field of cybernetics heralded by Norbert Weiner (another entropy aficionado) in the mid-twentieth century. As Frank and Wilson recount, "cybernetics assisted Tomkins in conceptualizing the human being as a loose assemblage of interrelated systems" (143). "These distinct systems (biological, psychological, sociological)," they continue, "are not reducible to one another but rather exist in relations of dependence on, as well as independence from, one another." Consequently, "Tomkins insists on a looseness of fit between and within systems, at all scales."[2] As Melissa Gregg and Gregory J. Seigworth phrase it, "With affect, a body is as much outside itself as in itself—webbed in its relations—until ultimately such firm distinctions cease to matter" (3). Affect accrues entropically, blurring the boundaries between emotional beings: "At once intimate and impersonal, affect *accumulates* across both relatedness and interruptions in relatedness, becoming a palimpsest of force-encounters traversing the ebbs and swells of

---

[2] Tomkins adds to the observable anatomical systems—cardiovascular, digestive, repository (which are indeed themselves implicated in the body's responses to affects)—"sub-systems within the personality" (*Shame* 175).

intensities that pass between 'bodies'" (2). Affect's accumulation is entropic, its accretion serving to dissolve intrapersonal and interpersonal obstructions of various kinds.

"Tomkins is most interested in the ways our affect theories are dynamic and interchangeable," according to Frank and Wilson: "'every theory, weak or strong, is in a relatively unstable equilibrium, which is constantly shifting.' A strong theory, for example, is built through endless processes of construction, destruction, and reconstruction" (98). This process is reminiscent of entropy. While disparate instances of deterioration do contribute to the final state of entropy writ large, heat death, individual cases remain in a sense isolated until that time. Therefore, the "reconstruction" stage of the construction-deconstruction-reconstruction process we see in Tomkins is reflected in the entropic process by virtue of what Rémy Lestienne calls a "disordered mixture":

> an undeniable parallel exists between the growth of a system's entropy and the disappearance of order. If a volume of gas divided among two communicating balloons contains a cold gas on one side and a hot gas on the other, the spontaneous evolution of the system leads to a mixture of uniform temperature. The initial order, in which the hot gas was found on one side and the cold gas on the other, has disappeared. In the same way, a drop of milk added to a cup of coffee diffuses, and this diffusion is accompanied by an augmentation of entropy. The initial 'order,' the milk on the one hand and the coffee on the other, dissolves into a disordered mixture. (119)

What we observe in "strong theory" creation is a recurrent process akin to entropy. Effort to resist a negative affect, shame, say, results not in relief but in the conversion of one affect into another, humiliation. Repeating this behavior ad nauseum leads to anger, itself fuel for the affects. If the human personality is a "perpetually open system," one permutation of this process forecasts further amplification of shame, further conversion of shame into humiliation, further anger at the feelings of humiliation (*Shame* 175). These experiences accumulate, potentially contaminating other systems.

Despite the absence of an overt incorporation of thermodynamic principles into Tomkins's expansive model of affect, one can't help but spot both cursory and consequential references to its principles in his writing.[3]

---

[3] For example, "So long as one is in the grip of a nuclear script," writes Tomkins, "one suffers an entropic malignancy which threatens the integrity of the personality" (*Shame* 195). More than a mere Easter egg, this reference illustrates how, as metaphor, entropy served

Although overselling the import of these references is not my objective, the language and reasoning he uses to construct his theories, and those others used to describe and explain them, frequently overlap with the mechanisms of entropy. To this end, I will highlight Tomkins's use of entropic concepts as part of his theories on anger and, an affect of particular importance, shame.

Anger most readily demonstrates this similitude. In ways visible and tangible, anger is a "hot affect": it causes a "reddening of the face which stimulates the heat receptors," and it increases blood pressure (*Shame* 197). In a sense, anger powers the other affects; it can "combine" with them and "intensify or modulate them, and suppress or reduce them" (198). Energy, too, can "intensify" and "suppress." Of course, energy is necessary for myriad useful processes. Yet, energy transfer compounds waste, which eventually overwhelms its system. Anger amplifies other affects, accelerating the accumulation of "experience" (165). "Cognitive hypersimplicity" and the "narrowing of the cognitive field" should also be mentioned here (206). Despite its chaotic implications, entropy is a monotonous process. It represents the degree to which useless energy accumulates because of a system's continual flow of thermal energy. This steady buildup is mirrored on the subjective level: "Excessive repetition of a single stimulus or single response is extremely satiating and punishing and finally angering" (205). Repetition experienced subjectively builds up to anger, which fuels the other affects. Writ large, this opens the door for the "possible entropic heat death" of one's "internal landscape" (206).

Moreover, affects cannot be done away with, only transformed into associated affects. Writing on humiliation trauma, Tomkins stages the hypothetical formation of a shame theory through an illustrative family drama that is both typical of his work and resonant with the Tyrone family's travails I discuss in Chap. 5. Tomkins's model reinforces the usefulness of imagining affects as energy: changeable, yet indestructible. As the family drama unfolds, a child and a playmate are slowly introducing disorder into their "life space" (*Shame* 176). The attendant parent attempts to calm and quiet the children so they will "stop accelerating the natural increase of general entropy." Though the "parent's irritation burns at a relatively slow rate," "impatience" soon exceeds "critical density": the

---

Tomkins when conceptualizing the boundaries of the personality. This remark reiterates his view of the various (sub)systems of the person as "containers with an inside and an outside" (Lakoff and Johnson 29).

parent lashes out physically, leaving the child "dissolved" in "tears." In entropic terms, Tomkins's drama presents a system altered by increased heat and thus increased entropy. Amidst accelerated entropy, the slow-burn of the parent's impatience converts into genuine anger. Heated, the parent compromises the child's own "life space," introducing shame. Since affects remain indefinitely, active or inert, this shame lingers, carrying the potential to amalgamate into a "theory":

> As the pool of information from stored past experience is brought to bear on the interpretation of input information, the number of alternative dimensions, and alternative selective interpretations of sub-sets of these dimensions, increase radically. When any stimulus in perceived … it may activate amplifying affect on an innate basis by virtue of the gradient and level of density of the neurological stimulation of the stimulus which is reported. It may also recruit from memory further information concerning past affects experienced when the same or similar stimuli were encountered before, which in turn may activate further affect. … After much cumulative experience, information about affects may become organized into what we term 'theories,' in much the same way that theories are constructed to account for uniformities in science or in cognition in general. An affect theory is a simplified and powerful summary of a larger set of affect experiences. (164–65)

As I remark above, waste energy builds up in a system because of the nature of heat exchange, which occurs in one direction only: from warmer to cooler. A comparable phenomenon manifests in affect theory construction when we replace waste energy with what Tomkins terms "isolated traces of past experience" (*Shame* 165). Once enough traces accumulate, they reach an equilibrium of a kind, codifying into a theory that becomes the dominant affect. "The existence of a shame theory," for example, "guarantees that the shame-relevant aspects of any situation will become figural in competition with other affect-relevant aspects of the same situations." A theory remains within a system indefinitely, altering its behavior ad infinitum.

The Permeability of Systems

The same qualities that make Tomkins's work puzzling make it proportionately provocative. One has the sense of experiencing hypotheses formation in medias res, a concurrent inward and outward blooming of ideas. As mentioned, Tomkins was influenced by cybernetics, heralded by

Norbert Weiner, in the mid-twentieth century. Tomkins consequently formed a "commitment to organized complexity"; that is, "conceptualizing relations among and between nested systems that are in some ways dependent on, and in other ways independent of, one another" (Frank and Wilson 74). This commitment pervades his work, but his devotion to cybernetic cogitation was both a boon and a blight. Case in point: on the one hand, Tomkins attests that the human personality is a "perpetually open system" (*Shame* 175); elsewhere he indicates the prospect of a person "unalloyed," a closed system, so to speak, wholly separate from external affect activators (150).[4] As Tomkins himself concedes, "any organized system is inherently ambiguous at its boundaries … at the most elementary particle or at the outer reaches of space at the time of the big bang" (qtd. in Frank and Wilson 167). If the affect system is a subsystem of the body, separate from the consciousness but nevertheless bound within and coterminous with the other systems of the body, this begs central questions of transferability and dominance. To comprehensively observe any system, its boundaries need demarcation. The shame affect is useful in establishing a controlling typography for the following relationships: (1) the affects in relation to each other; (2) the affects in relation to the conscious self; (3) the body in relation to the outside world.

Eve Kosofsky Sedgwick and Adam Frank outline a perimeter around the affects in relation to each other through a look at shame, the "exemplary affect for theory" (21). Shame is special in that, unlike most other affects that are "activated by a certain 'frequency of neural firing per unit time' represented by a straight line of some (positive, negative, or zero) slope, shame, like disgust and contempt, is activated by the drawing of a boundary line or barrier, the 'introduc[tion] of a particular boundary or frame into an analog continuum.' That is, shame involves a gestalt, the duck to interest's (or enjoyment's) rabbit" (22). Shame is dependent on the erstwhile activation of other affects:

> Without positive affect, there can be no shame: only a scene that offers you enjoyment or engages your interest can make you blush. Similarly, only something you thought might delight or satisfy can disgust. Both these affects produce bodily knowledges: disgust, as spitting out bad-tasting food,

---

[4] However: (1) to occupy this state is implausible, given that to enjoy it one must inhabit a system perfectly attuned to individual excitement and interest; and (2) affects can be activated independently of outside motivators (*Shame* 150).

recognizes the difference between inside and outside the body and what should and should not be let in; shame, as precarious hyperreflexivity of the surface of the body, can turn one inside out—or outside in .... Shame is one of those affects whose digitalizing mechanism works to 'punctuat[e the system] as distinct.' Perhaps, along with contempt and disgust, it can be a switch point for the individuation of imaging systems, of consciousnesses, of bodies, of theories, of selves, and individuation that decides not necessarily an identity but a figuration, distinction, or mark of punctuation. And unlike contempt or disgust, shame is characterized by its failure ever to renounce its object cathexis, its relation to the desire for pleasure as well as the need to avoid pain. (22–23)

Shame's activation is cartographic: it delimits its own boundaries and the boundaries of its neighboring affects. In doing so, shame can serve to safeguard the condition of the adjacent affects and the body. This partition serves to isolate shame within the affect system, but the ameliorative benefits are offset by shame's regressive tendency to reactivate. The above example helps us imagine a topography of the affect system: all affects are housed within the affect system; some affects—shame (and disgust and contempt)—are activated through the circumscription of a defining boundary around shame; shame's boundary, at the same time, demarcates the boundaries of the contiguous affects. Therefore, we proceed with the knowledge that the affect system is porous, susceptible to the influence of input originating inside and outside of the affect system itself.[5]

"In contrast to all other affects," writes Tomkins, "shame is an experience of the self by the self" (*Shame* 136). If all desired objects originated externally, one might shelter one's consciousness from shame indefinitely. Objects of excitement, in truth, can be one's own "body" or "self" (150). In the absence of external shame activators, one's inability to act on one's wants, for instance, activates shame. "[R]elevant stimulus for the affect system includes internal as well as external events, concluding firmly that there is no basis ... for a definitional distinction between response and stimulus" (Sedgwick and Frank 11). There exists no means to harbor the

---

[5] Tomkins's "multiple negative affect bind" implies a similarly rigid delineation of affects: in this case, an affect is "controlled and bound by many other negative affects" (*Shame* 177). Every "attempt to minimize or escape the shameful situation" results in the "original shame amplified." Though one's struggle may result in evading authentic shame, its amplified form, "anguished humiliation," endures. Regardless, shame can't be eliminated, only converted.

consciousness from affects activated by internal motivators. Therefore, while distinct from the affect system, the consciousness is pervious to its influence. Tomkins's "cybernetic model of neural communication," abridged below, helps us imagine the contours that circumscribe the self within the outside world:

> 'We conceive of man ... as an inter and intra-communication system, utilizing feedback networks which transmit, match and transform, information in analogical form and in the form of messages in a language. By a communication system we mean a mechanism capable of regular and systematic duplication of something in space and time.' In humans and other organisms, sensory receptors duplicate 'certain aspects of the world surrounding the receptors,' and this information, primarily in analog form, is then duplicated again and again via afferent nerves and transmitted further into the organism. In mobile and more complex organisms, there is a receiving station at which there occurs an additional kind of duplication, 'an as yet unknown process we will call *transmuting*,' that turns the analog information into a conscious report. (Frank and Wilson 81–82)

Organisms, then, receive input from the outside, which is then dispersed within through a system capable of "duplication." Humans, of course, also possess consciousness, "a unique type of duplication by which some aspects of the world reveal themselves to another part of the same world' (qtd. in Frank and Wilson 82); this is so thanks to the enigmatic process of "transmuting," or the process by which input comes to be cognizance. This being the case, Tomkins "avoids a transcendentalizing break or cut between consciousness and the world. He ... maintains continuity between consciousness and its objects" (Frank and Wilson 82). This detail suggests no separation between the self that perceives and the object of perception, therefore indicating the absence of a barrier between self and world.[6]

---

[6] Elsewhere, however, Tomkins upholds an opposing "discontinuity between organism and environment" (Frank and Wilson 84). He "insists on one of the basic tenets of biological systems theory—that the distinction between organism and environment reappears and is made use of within the organism itself" (84). We return to the shame affect to clarify these matters. Shame is elicited when "barriers" debar one from "objects of excitement and enjoyment" (*Shame* 150). That is: (1) I desire excitement activated by an "object" outside myself; (2) something prevents the acquisition; (3) shame, externally motivated, activates internally at the withholding; (4) though affectively changed, I remain effectively separate from both the "object" and the world we share.

Empathic and Vicarious Shame

Shame helps us establish a controlling typography for the affects in relation to each other and the conscious self, as well as for the body in relation to the outside world.[7] But how does understanding this help us interpret modernist literature? Because of how shame functions intra- and interpersonally, it gives us a fresh way to view literary characters, their behaviors, and their interactions. It is true that shame is a predominately negative affect, which raises considerable questions if we consider its link to "identification" (*Shame* 139). Hope lies in the fact that, though an "impediment to intimacy and communion," shame is not a permanent state. The concept of "empathic shame" carries social and political implications that are reproduced within the personal spheres encompassing friends and loved ones:

> In a democratically organized society the belief that all men are created equal means that all men are possible objects of identification. When one man expresses contempt for another, the other is more likely to experience shame than self-contempt insofar as the democratic ideal has been internalized. This is because he assumes that ultimately he will wish to commune with this one who is expressing contempt and that this wish is mutual. Contempt will be used sparingly in a democratic society lest it undermine solidarity, whereas it will be used frequently and with approbation in a hierarchically organized society in order to maintain distance between individuals, classes, and nations. In a democratic society, contempt will often be replaced by empathic shame, in which the critic hangs his head in shame at what the other has done, or by distress in which the critic expresses his suffering at what the other has done, or by anger in which the critic seeks redress for the wrongs committed by the other.
>
> The polarization between the democratic and hierarchically organized society with respect to shame and contempt holds also in families and socialization within democratic and hierarchically organized societies. (139–40)

In this summation, acts of contempt bear the capacity to activate "empathic shame" in the target of contempt. This is due to the prognostication that results from the "democratic ideal ... internalized," which causes the target of contempt to realize that this schism is only a temporary separation preceding what will ultimately be the mutually desired communion of

---

[7] In this section, I use the terms "shame" and "shame-humiliation" interchangeably since their relationship is explained above.

both parties. So, we see how shame is transferable through the act of contempt. One is also susceptible to "the vicarious experience of shame": "the human being is capable through empathy and identification of living through others and therefore of being shamed by what happens to others" (*Shame* 159). Thus, one's potential for vicarious shame is relative to the degree to which one cathects with the other people and "institutions" that comprise one's world.

Shame is dependent on positive affects. This aspect is crucial for understanding shame and its applications. Like the construction-deconstruction-reconstruction process we see in "strong theory" formation, mutual shame "strengthens any social group and its sense of community":

> Just as contempt strengthens the boundaries and barriers between individuals and groups and is the instrument par excellence for the preservation of hierarchical, caste, and class relationships, so is shared shame a prime instrument for strengthening the sense of mutuality and community whether it be between parent and child, friend and friend, or citizen and citizen. When one is ashamed of the other, that other is not only forced into shame but he is also reminded that the other is sufficiently concerned positively as well as negatively to feel ashamed of and for the other. (*Shame* 156–57)

As discussed above, shame "is activated by the drawing of a boundary line or barrier"; shared or empathic shame serves to enlarge the circle so encompassed, in essence welcoming the other to share a communal space. Shame "enlarges the spectrum of objects" that can "engage" or "concern" one (*Shame* 162). Therefore, one's system, one's area of influence, grows through the communal experience of shame. This phenomenon has lingering effects: once one has experienced empathy thusly, one "will never again be able to be entirely unconcerned with the other." That Tomkins thinks in cycles is apparent: "empathy is a necessary condition for the development of personality and civilization alike[;] it is also a necessary condition for the experience of shame. If there is insufficient interest in the other, shame through empathy is improbable. How much shame can be felt at remediable conditions is one critical measure of the stage of development of any civilization." This is hard to imagine. There must be a beginning and an end, an "inside and an outside." This is where thinking about affect entropically is essential: instead of a shame-empathy cycle or paradox, we can imagine a shame-empathy process, one that is "dynamic and changeable," but with a conclusion.

Character and Identification

Empathy is a common human trait: "earliest speech is an empathic act, a wish to do what the other is doing rather than communicate something to the other" (*Shame* 91).[8] Empathy has been used as a metric for the humanity of fictional characters. The well-known example Suzanne Keen uses is a good one. In the filmic version of Philip K. Dick's *Do Androids Dream of Electric Sheep*—*Blade Runner*—virtually human cyborgs are outwitted by their inability to convincingly imitate human empathy. Had the cyborgs been able to show empathy, they would have been considered (more) human, within the world of *Blade Runner*. Does this mean that fictional characters can achieve varying degrees of humanness? Felski claims that "Characters do not have to be deep, well-rounded, psychologically complex, or unified to count as characters …. They need only to be *animated*: to act and react, to will and intend" (78). The value of a fictional world is routinely judged by the breadth and execution of its character development; that is, how convincingly a character mirrors an actual person, how plausibly the character's story unfolds. No character is fully developed upon introduction; it is a process that implicates not least author, character, reader/viewer.

That fictional characters *are* actual humans is not the argument I, or anyone, really, is making. That said, aren't characters simply underdeveloped, so to speak, in one way or another? Like entropy or theory formation, development is accumulative:

> Every life history has a theme, but it is truly indeterminate until the entire melody has appeared and been repeated often enough so that the individual can recognize it, construct it, and then begin to recognize further repetitions of it as he develops. The young human is a relatively open system, because each new experience plays a vital role in the interpretation of the growing cumulative images of past experience. (*Shame* 122)

---

[8] Keen provides a useful summation of empathy, a neologism arising at the turn of the century meaning "a vicarious, spontaneous sharing of affect, [that] can be provoked by witnessing another's emotional state, by hearing about another's condition, or even by reading … . Equipped with mirror neurons, the human brain appears to possess a system for automatically sharing feelings, what neuroscientists call a 'shared manifold for intersubjectivity'" (4). Thus, we add amongst all other bodily systems what we might call the empathy system.

Once born, a child is considered *human* at age three, age five, age twelve, even though the child is undergoing a process of development that will continue for many more years. One does not achieve human status at a certain point in this process. Societies do differentiate between, for example, children and adults, but one's humanity is not the source of debate.

If "fictional worlds provide safe zones for readers' feeling empathy without experiencing a resultant demand on real-world action," is this not the case for fictional characters? (Keen 4). Moi concedes that, although characters are invented "pieces of writing ... that come alive in our minds" (55), to make connections with them is only natural: "To respond to fictional characters with emotions (and so on) is just what we do" (59). It is the world-creation that most interests Moi, not so much the ontological status of its inhabitants: "Above all: description conjures up a world for the reader. A text is not a set of signifiers ... in search of a meaning. A literary text gives us a world. The task of literacy criticism is not to reduce that world to pure form but to account for it in its full complexity, including its forms" (68). In the end, it is precisely the representation of possible empathic experiences between fictional characters that communicates empathy to the reader as "a representational goal" (Keen 121).

To clarify, my argument in the chapters to follow is not meant to establish an empathic link between readers and characters. This has been well-accomplished by Keen, Vermeule, and others.[9] Not only this, focusing on identification allows us to sidestep the hazy relationship between empathy and sympathy (also covered in Keen).[10] My emphasis is on instances of characters showing empathic tendencies *for other characters*. Given the "porous ... boundaries between texts and everyday life" (Felksi 86), identification is merely a side effect for the reader:

---

[9] See Vermeule, Blakey. *Why Do We Care about Literary Characters?* Johns Hopkins University Press (2010).

[10] Empathy and sympathy are not perfectly interchangeable: "On most accounts, sympathy differs from empathy by being triggered solely by emotions that are linked with pain and involves—either as consequence or through sharing the other person's pain—feeling sorry for the other person or wanting to alleviate the other person's suffering. The phrases feeling with and feeling for, respectively, are often used to capture the difference between the two notions" (Deonna 344). Furthermore, "Empathy may more briefly be defined as the self-conscious awareness of the consciousness of others ... . Empathy, unlike sympathy, denotes an active referent. In empathy one attends to the feelings of another; in sympathy one attends to the suffering of another, but the feelings are one's own. In empathy I try to feel your pain. In sympathy I know you are in pain, and I sympathize with you, but I feel my sympathy and my pain, not your anguish and your pain" ("Sympathy and Empathy" 441).

> Identification ... implies a sense of something shared, but this does not mean obliterating or overriding differences .... To identify with something is not to be identical with it; we are talking about the rough ground of resemblance rather than pure sameness .... [I]dentifying does not simply entrench a prior self but may enrich, expand, or amend it. Perhaps we glimpse aspects of ourselves in a character, but in a way that causes us to revise our sense of who we are. (80–81)

In another iteration of the "construction-deconstruction-reconstruction" process, the "'shock of recognition'" prompts the dismantling of the self and, subsequently, a reorganizing of the self in an upgraded form (81). One reason this back-and-forth between character and person is seamless is that we share an Umwelt: "the dynamic and open-ended nature of a being's relation to its surroundings ... [T]he environment as it concerns us is a networked array of phenomena. Characters matter to *us* and yet are not simply 'in our minds'; they come to us as if from elsewhere; they possess a degree of solidity, permanence, and force" (87). It is not so much that we connect empathically with characters as it is that we "connect *through* them to other persons" (90). Therefore, if we witness characters behaving empathically to one another, we may identify with them and—through them—connect empathically with those actual persons in our lives. Finally, I must address that modernist literature, the period that "dealt a death blow to character," presents considerable hurdles to the present study (91). But, as I have shown above, if character in modernism is "shredded, dissolved, and washed away," this is but one step in a process of rebuilding (92).

> No one would dispute that fictional figures look different in [modernism] ... Yet this does not mean that person schemas drop out of sight or that readers do not form ties to figures in modernist fiction. The twofoldedness of character—as both person and aesthetic device—is manifest in [modernism] .... [W]e might want to make a case not just for the twofoldedness of character but for its multifoldedness. (92)

If an "algorithmic" look at affect will unveil the "middle ranges of affective agency," we can do the same for character in modernism. Of course, modernism was meant to be a conscious break with its past, but what of its present? In the chapters below, I show that amidst destruction, there was a simultaneous effort to rebuild. I concentrate on four primary texts spanning the fin de siècle to World War II. A chronological approach shows how each author's treatment of entropy and affect evolves alongside the attitude and writing of the era, from an optimistic naturalist origin to a tragic end. What's more, these texts are of special interest in regards to character and identification in their connection to the real world through their characters: Stephen Crane's 1898 short story "The Open Boat" is based loosely on his own shipwreck experience; the abolitionist John Brown haunts Jean Toomer's 1922 short story "Withered Skin of Berries"; Virginia Woolf's memory of her mother permeates her 1927 novel *To the Lighthouse*; and, written during the early years of World War II, *Long Day's Journey into Night* presents a tragic family drama reminiscent of Eugene O'Neill's own.

WORKS CITED

Bell, Ian F. A. "The Real and the Ethereal: Modernists Energies in Eliot and Pound." *From Energy to Information*, edited by Bruce Clarke and Linda Dalrymple Henderson. Stanford University Press, 2002, pp. 114–25.

Felksi, Rita. "Identifying with Characters." *Character: Three Inquiries in Literary Studies*. University of Chicago Press, 2019, pp. 77–126.

Frank, Adam J. and Elizabeth A. Wilson. *A Silvan Tomkins Handbook: Foundations for Affect Theory*. University of Minnesota Press, 2020. *Project MUSE* muse.jhu.edu/book/78624.

Fraser, Graham. "The Fall of the House of Ramsay: Virginia Woolf's Ahuman Aesthetics of Ruin." *Criticism: A Quarterly for Literature and the Arts*, vol. 62, no. 1, 2020, pp. 117–141. EBSCOhost, http://search.ebscohost.com/login.aspx?direct=true&db=mzh&AN=202019534468&site=ehost-live.

James, David. "Affect's Vocabularies: Literature and Feeling after 1890." *The New Modernist Studies*, edited by Douglas Mao. Cambridge University Press, 2021.

Keen, Suzanne. *Empathy and the Novel*. Oxford University Press, 2007.

Lakoff, George and Mark Johnson. *Metaphors We Live By*. The University of Chicago Press, 1980.

Lestienne, Remy. "The Age of Things, Order and Chaos, Entropy and Information." *The Children of Time: Causality, Entropy, Becoming*. Translated by E. C. Neher. University of Illinois Press, 1995, pp. 119.

Meisel, Martin. *Chaos Imagined: Literature, Art, Science*. Columbia University Press, 2016.

Moi, Toril. "Rethinking Character." *Character: Three Inquiries in Literary Studies*. University of Chicago Press, 2019, pp. 27–75.

Morrisson, Mark S. "The Physical Sciences and Mathematics." *Modernism, Science, and Technology*. Bloomsbury Publishing, 2016. *ProQuest Ebook Central*, https://ebookcentral-proquest.com.libproxy.uncg.edu/lib/uncg/detail.action?docID=4605643, pp. 37–82.

Murray, Cara. "Cultivating Chaos: Entropy, Information, and the Making of the *Dictionary of National Biography.*" *Victorian Literature and Culture*, vol. 50, no. 1, 2022, pp. 87–116. *EBSCOhost*, https://doi-org.libproxy.uncg.edu/10.1017/S1060150320000121.

Nicholls, Marcus. "The Adaptive Afterlife of Texts: Entropy and Generative Decay." *Adaptation*, vol. 14, no. 3, 2021, pp. 313–334, https://doi.org.libproxy.uncg.edu/10.1093/adaptation/apab001.

Phillips, Matt. "Entropy and Equilibrium in Jean Toomer's *Cane.*" *Mississippi Quarterly*, vol. 74 no. 2, 2021, p. 203–225. *Project MUSE*, https://doi.org/10.1353/mss.2022.0004.

Sausman, Justin. "From Vibratory Occultism to Vibratory Modernism: Blackwood, Lawrence, Woolf." *Vibratory Modernism*, edited by Anthony Enns and Shelley Trower, Palgrave Macmillan, 2013, pp. 30–52.

Scruggs, Charles and Lee VanDemarr. *Jean Toomer and the Terrors of American History*. University of Pennsylvania Press, 1998.

Seigworth, Gregory J. and Melissa Gregg. "An Inventory of Shimmers." *The Affect Theory Reader*, edited by Melissa Gregg and Gregory J. Seigworth. Duke University Press, 2010, pp. 1–25.

Taylor, Julie. "Introduction: Modernism and Affect." *Modernism and Affect*, edited by Julie Taylor. Edinburgh University Press, 2015, p. 2.

Tomkins, Silvan. *Shame and its Sisters*, edited by Eve Kosofsky Sedgwick and Adam Frank. Duke University Press, 1995.

———. "The Quest for Primary Motives: Biography and Autobiography of an Idea." *Journal of Personality and Social Psychology*, vol. 41, no. 2, 1981, pp. 306–29.

Toomer, Jean. *A Jean Toomer Reader*, edited by Frederick L. Rusch Oxford University Press, 1993.

Watkins, Megan. "Desiring Recognition, Accumulating Affect." *The Affect Theory Reader*, edited by Melissa Gregg and Gregory J. Seigworth. Duke University Press, 2010, pp. 296–85.

Wraith, Matthew. "Throbbing Human Engines: Mechanical Vibration, Entropy and Death in Marinetti, Joyce, Ehrenburg, and Eliot." *Vibratory Modernism*, edited by Anthony Enns and Shelley Trower, Palgrave Macmillan, 2013, pp. 96–114.

CHAPTER 2

Writing as Rescue in Stephen Crane's "The Open Boat"

Abstract Stephen Crane's 1898 short story "The Open Boat," based loosely on the author's own shipwreck experience, prefigures much of what would become standard in modernist literature: distrust, confusion, and a desperate exploration of art's potential for humanity. The story represents a twofold act of self-preservation for Crane, who not only creates a safe zone where, through identification with his fictitious persona, he relives his own shipwreck experience from a secure distance, but also, in withholding identification, leaves readers open to what Silvan Tomkins calls "empathic shame," a communal affect that deems readers "interpreters" of the limits of individualism within a healthy democracy.

Keywords Crane, Stephen • Disorder • Equilibrium • Energy • Empathy • Entropy • Heat death • "The Open Boat"

Stephen Crane published his short story "The Open Boat" (1898) at a time of waning, as his present century, and his own short life, approached conclusion. One detects this sense of decline in his work. Crane's writing reflects an interest in subjectivity within an indifferent universe. His poems' speakers, for example, reveal the worth of individual interpretation when one's presence inspires no "sense of obligation" in whatever higher

© The Author(s), under exclusive license to Springer Nature Switzerland AG 2025
M. Phillips, *Disorder, Affect, and Modernist Literature*, Palgrave Studies in Affect Theory and Literary Criticism,
https://doi.org/10.1007/978-3-031-92463-7_2

power may reside over the cosmos (Katz 102). The indifference, or nonexistence, of a controlling power dictates that one's perspective of the world—one's reading—defines it. Even so, in the world of "The Open Boat," Crane's confounding narrative technique and unsteady prose disorient the reader, calling into question means of identification and any potential "safe zones" available to the reader (Keen 4). Crane does not encourage the reader to identify with the crew in any traditional sense. Instead, the story represents a twofold act of self-preservation. Crane not only creates for himself a "safe zone" where, through identification with his fictitious persona, he relives his own shipwreck experience from a secure distance; but in withholding identification, he also leaves readers open to "empathic shame" (*Shame* 139), a communal affect that deems readers "interpreters" of the limits of individualism within a healthy democracy (Crane 144).

The story depicts the plight of four shipwreck survivors at odds with the forces of nature. The correspondent, Crane's persona, is accompanied by the captain, cook, and oiler, Billie Higgins, the only crew member given a name. Crane survived a shipwreck under similar conditions, which suggests an autobiographical component. This piece prefigures much of what would become the emblems of modernism: distrust of past constructs' ability to provide a way forward and the confusion that results from being so unmoored; an exploration of the potential of art to mollify and act as surrogate. A resident of Greenwich Village around the turn of the century, Crane is one of the many "literary radicals" who influence the next generation of writers drawn to the progressive politics and literacy production in bohemian New York (Scruggs and VanDemarr 47). Crane's themes of depersonalization and his bleak depictions of war prefigure similar sentiments from modern poets such as Siegfried Sassoon, Wilfred Owen, and Ivor Gurney. The picture Crane paints in "The Open Boat" provides a template that is followed in the following years in works such as Conrad's *Heart of Darkness*, the existentialist writing of Sartre, and Beckett's absurdist theater. Frederick Hoffman argues that Crane "was the only genuine predecessor of the 1920s generation of writers" (55). Thomas Claviez calls Crane "intermediate, in that he occupies a position between Whitman's romanticism and of the American self and the modernism of someone like Wallace Stevens" (140). Crane complicates the "role of the omniscient narrator" with a "semantics of doubt" (145). The "faces of the men must have been grey. Their eyes must have glinted in strange ways as they gazed steadily astern," we read (Crane 123). Like a scene from *Endgame*, the crew are crammed in the small vessel, ignorant of what surrounds them. Readers are equally unsure.

Crane's narrative instability begs questions of reader identification. As stated, Suzanne Keen posits that "fictional worlds provide safe zones for readers' feeling empathy without experiencing a resultant demand on real-world action" (4). But what if the reader is left high and dry in an unstable environment that confuses their propinquity to author and text? The sea is, after all, many things. Regina Schober claims that, as a "metaphorical realm," it's a place where writers can "experiment with tropes such as the confrontation between human beings and their environment, the search for an inaccessibility of knowledge amidst the chaos of inundating data, the emergent and thus unpredictable manifestations of large-scale knowledge systems, and the unattainability of individual integrity and self-knowledge" (71). To merely go out to sea is to subject oneself to increased disorder. The crew's survival requires the continuous and often intuited teamwork of the men under the enduring guidance of the injured captain. The "shore" possesses a certain "immovable quality," compared to the "confusion of the sea" (Crane 142). "In a simple social situation like that of the boat," writes John J. Conder, "instinct to survive easily creates a sense of the right and leads to brotherhood because all the men can readily enough perceive the common threat posed by the sea. Such a shared perception makes absurdly clear the moral demands of brotherhood, cooperation, and obligation" (29). The crew experience a range of affects, not least shame and anger. Add to this that seafaring per se magnifies feeling. Tony Tanner explains it this way:

> [T]he ship creates a special 'fellowship' among and between all who sail in her. On land, people have an endless variety of commitments, relationships, obligations, loyalties, and so on; at sea, everyone—it has entered into common parlance—is 'in the same boat.' And that boat is a lifeboat at all times breasting and seeking to avoid death-by-water. The intensity of the 'fellowship' which thus ensues, or is thereby created (and the possible strains within it), is thus considerably heightened, and sharpened, and *tested*. ("Introduction" xii)

This nautical phenomenon corresponds with "Cognitive hypersimplicty" and the "narrowing of the cognitive field" in Tomkins (*Shame* 206). Anger can amplify other affects. Despite its chaotic implications, entropy is a monotonous process. The same is true of shipwreck, "*apropos* of nothing"

(Crane 127). "Excessive repetition of a single stimulus or single response is extremely satiating and punishing and finally angering," writes Tomkins (*Shame* 205). Repetition experienced subjectively builds up to anger, "possible strains," say, which fuels the other affects. Writ large, this opens the door for the "possible entropic heat death" of one's "internal landscape" (206). Hence, the crew is vulnerable to a subjective mirroring of their environment, a shipwreck of the self. In such an unruly system, then, one becomes open to new avenues of experience and returns (one hopes) to land changed. That said, if "empathy is a necessary condition for … civilization," how much empathy is experienced amidst an uninhabitable shipwreck? (162). "If there is insufficient interest in the other," argues Tomkins, "shame through empathy is improbable." Therefore, if any of the crew lack sufficient "interest" in the other, contempt, not shame, will activate for them. While shame is communal, contempt "is a powerful instrument of discrimination and segregation" (158).

Benjamin Ives Gilman sets out to evangelize the developing aesthetic implications of empathy in 1924. The creation and appreciation of art, he explains, require the artist and its viewer to enter a distinctive emotional space marked by a "mood of self-forgetfulness under the influence of admiration" (15). Artists breach this space while creating; the viewer while observing. For Gilman, empathy is "a beholder's reproduction of the mood of absorption in which a work of art beheld was conceived." This "mood," what Gilman calls "ecstasy," reveals empathy-as-art's connections with entropy: "We combine two Greek vocables—one the preposition *ek*, out of, and the other the noun *stasis*, or standing—in the word ecstasy … . [T]he mood of the artist in conceiving … is one of ecstasy—the mood in which the thing we behold is for the moment all there is to us." The work of art, then, is born out of stasis, the final stage of the entropic process. In an aesthetics that privileges stasis, more entropy, as a matter of course, correlates with more "ecstasy." As one chooses the sufferings of the sea over the relief of the land, the artist and viewer must step outside of their system and into another to experience empathy-as-art.

A century on, Toril Moi's and Rita Felski's recent analyses of character identification reaffirm Gilman's argument. Moi stresses that "A literary text gives us a world" (68). Given the "porous … boundaries between texts and everyday life," as Felski puts it, identification is merely a side effect for the reader (86). Therefore, if we witness characters behaving empathically to one another, we may identify with them and—through them—connect empathically with those actual persons around us. These sentiments echo Gilman's "mood of self-forgetfulness under the influence of admiration" (15). The author creates the world-as-text, and the reader visits this world by reading. The experience is one of stasis (ecstasy) in that it is stable. For Gilman, a crucial component of the artistic process is providing the work of art an enduring form: "there is more to the mood of the artist in *producing* his work than ecstasy; for he is busied at giving permanent form to his conception; or more explicitly, at fashioning an outward thing which when it is contemplated will revive his mood in conceiving it." The artist must simultaneously create and cross over into the space generative of the artwork; not only this, but also give the artwork, and the space, permanent form.

As we know, "Open Boat" was prompted by Crane's own shipwreck. His metamorphosis from writer to reader is only natural. It just so happens that the space he inhabited to create his work of art—his story—exists interstitially, somewhere between the physical/geographic and the intellectual/emotional. Crane, of course, would not expect his readers to survive a shipwreck for his point to be taken, and the shipwreck itself is not the point. The chaos of the wreck created an impermanent, inimitable space that Crane would later be tasked to recreate in permanent form, to make accessible to not only his imagined reader but to himself. Crane can return to that place through identification with his fictitious persona, the correspondent.

The setting of Crane's story indicates the late stages of the entropic process: "it was not difficult to imagine that [a] particular wave was the final outburst of the ocean, the last effort of the grim water" (123). The sea is bleak and grey, but also "free," "wild with lights of emerald and white and amber" (124). From the start, Crane depicts the crew not only physically but intellectually linked, as "all … knew the colours of the sea" (121). The crew's aptitude for information exchange likewise degrades: they argue, complain, and speak in "disjointed sentences" (123). Matthew Wraith writes about the relationship between communication and entropy:

> A *decrease* in the order and efficiency of a system can sometimes mean an increase in its potential to convey information.
>
> Communication involves the reduction of noise—of informational entropy. Information is necessarily *negentropic*: it orders the random stochastic distribution of sounds (or whatever medium) into an improbable

pattern. But it also requires a *certain amount* of entropy, a certain loss of pattern, to do its work. Perfect predictability and pattern tells us nothing we don't already know … . In other words, a system can *decay into signification*. (107–08)

Wraith claims that there is potential for a balance between a system's overall order and its potential for useful communication exchange. Crane illustrates such potential in his story, as the crew attempt to negotiate their entropic surroundings, both intellectually and physically. For example, their means of communication as well as their ability for physical expression is stifled: "anything resembling an emphatic gesture would have capsized" the craft (124). Billie is key when discussing a sense of balance in the story. While the others are nearly absorbed into their surroundings, Billie strives to maintain what we might call the initial order. At the beginning of the story, Billie's focus is outward, while the correspondent and captain are introspective. The correspondent "wondered why he was there"; Billie "raised himself suddenly to keep clear of water" (122). Billie rejects surrender, attempting to maintain his slippery hold on the familiarity of his previous environment. We sense Billie's anxiety, but anxiety serves only to add to the nervous energy accumulating in the system. Crane calls this phenomenon a "singular disadvantage of the sea" which "lies in the fact that after successfully surmounting one wave you discover that there is another behind it" (122). Repetition, too, forecasts total predictability in the system.

Crane's repetition emphasizes the accumulation of entropy in the system. The crew merge more intensely as the story progresses. Even the barriers separating Billie from the rest of the crew begin to dissolve. Crane demonstrates this by virtue of the characters' interchangeability, as well as in the predictability of his prose: "In the meantime the oiler and the correspondent rowed. And also they rowed. They sat together in the same seat, and each rowed an oar. Then the oiler took both oars; then the correspondent took both oars; then the oiler, then the correspondent. They rowed and they rowed" (125). Crane shows how empathic merging provides benefits for the crew. For example, it allows them to share the last remnants of heat in a system nearing equilibrium. The bond shared by the men takes on quasi-corporeal form: "It would be difficult to describe the subtle brotherhood of men that was here established on the seas … . But it dwelt in the boat, and each man felt it warm him" (126). As one, the crew can survive, for a time, by the last vestiges of warmth in their system.

The empathy they experience deepens significantly, going beyond a "mere recognition of what was best for the common safety. There was surely in it a quality that was personal and heartfelt" (126). The system's entropic conditions dissolve all boundaries, physical, intellectual, emotional, and social, shown in the fact that the correspondent "who had been taught to be cynical of men" viewed his present conditions as the "best experience of his life" (126).

A developing sense of empathy among the crew is beneficial, but it is not enough to ensure their survival. The "little grey shadow" of the distant lighthouse provides the crew with something to strive for, but conditions continually degenerate around their craft (126). The waves continue to bash the boat anxiously and repetitively, washing away distinctions between crewmates: the "oiler or the correspondent took the oars" (127). Crane makes known the limits of the highly pressurized version of empathy the sea engenders. Remarkably, as the bonds between the men in the boat increase, their connection to the people outside of their current system strains. The crew's mutual disdain for those "who thought it amusing to row a boat" brings the oiler and the correspondent to a place of "full sympathy" (127). Hating those back on land, however, is wasted energy. The captain warns, "'Don't spend yourselves,'" but Billie, in particular, flouts this order (127). "Billie fights against the unseen forces," Max L. Autry attests, "the fates, and does not seek, request, or accept assistance … . Chance or fate, factors beyond man's control, offers help to the crew, and the other three humble themselves in the fact of a greater force … and are saved. Billie does not, and dies" (107). As the crew fight against the waves that draw them further and further from land, they continue judging all those who still dwell on the shore. Out on the dinghy, their minds are "sharpened"; those on shore are the picture of "incompetency and blindness and, indeed, cowardice" (Crane 129). The crew pride themselves on courage. Hoffman comments on Crane's commitment to courage, the namesake of his best-known novel, *The Red Badge of Courage*. He observes that it was Crane's "exhaustive, almost obsessive, examination of courage" that earned his novel the "respect" of the writers to follow him in the 1920s:

> Crane described courage as the consequence of an accident, wholly removed from the glamourous circumstances traditionally supposed to accompany it. For [the writers after Crane], courage was a word used to signify an instinctive move toward or away from the center of violence, with self-preservation

and self-respect the mixed motives. It was not, in fact, an emotion at all—certainly not in the sense of governing an act or preparing a man for the performance of one. (56)

Courage in Crane, then, is little more than primitive self-preservation borne from an evolutionary imperative. This sort of perfunctory grab at survival results in Billie's death.

Billie betrays Crane's views on individualism. The crew's waning hope of rescue stirs "rage" in them (Crane 129). Action, however, will not produce the desired result. In a system close to stasis, all energy expenditure adds to already accumulating waste energy. Shivering is a good example. Wraith discusses shivering, what he terms the "ultimate form of entropic vibration" in comparison to the vibration of engines:

> Engine vibration is a form of entropy. It is an inefficiency in the system; part of the ineradicable portion of an engine's expenditure of energy that is rendered unavailable for useful work. Shivering is the ultimate form of entropic vibration because its purpose is precisely to turn the chaotic, but still perceptible movement of vibration into the even more chaotic molecular agitation that can be felt as heat and constitutes the terminal state of all energy. We shiver to preserve ourselves, to try to maintain our warm-blooded homeostasis. But in doing do, we merely hasten our own entropic decay. (100)

In our own universe, we can subsist despite performing wasteful actions such as shivering, for a time. We get cold, we shiver, we feel warmer. But actions such as these produce waste energy, the store of which will be responsible for the (supposed) eventual heat death of the universe. In the closed system that Crane creates, however, everything is intensified such that entropy's effects are more immediate. As the system closes in around them, the crew perform wasteful work, worsening their circumstances: "The shadows on the sea slowly deepened. The wind bore coldness with it, and the men began to shiver" (Crane 133). The bleak reality that the crew only exacerbate their anguish by trying to keep warm is central to Crane's pessimistic depiction of the human condition.

Crane's self-preservation is mirrored in the correspondent. Left with no other means of escape, poetry emerges from the deep recesses of the correspondent's mind. Apropos of Gilman, Caroline Sheridan Norton's "Bingen on the Rhine" created a realm theretofore nonexistent and gave it permanent form; hence, her poem's admirer enters this realm when experiencing the poem.[1] The correspondent, then, can retreat into this place; indeed, so convincingly so that he "plainly [sees] the soldier" (138). The "soldier's plight" now comes to the correspondent as a "human, living thing" (138). The correspondent, having identified with the soldier, experiences a flowering of empathy for the rest of the crew. This same reliance on one's neighbor, which Billie rejects, saves the correspondent, the cook, and the captain in the end.

Crane shows that a change has taken place thanks to the correspondent's experience with art. The correspondent understands that he must escape this place and make it back to his previous system. The correspondent's consciousness-altering experience with art is followed by a "slow and gradual disentanglement" that ultimately separates Billie from the rest of the men (138). Here in this system's "last stages of exhaustion," the men begin to develop a sort of immunity to the sea: "spray occasionally ... gave them a fresh soaking, but this had no power to break their repose. The ominous slash of the wind and the water affected them as it would have affected mummies" (139). Their flesh seems rigid, no longer permeable. The intellectual link between the crew, too, deteriorates, the "full meaning of their glances ... shrouded" (141). In fact, conscious processes cease for the correspondent, his "mind ... dominated ... by the muscles" (141). The men communicate and act habitually. Autrey writes the following:

> [A] meaningful distinction is soon drawn between the oiler and his three comrades. All but Billie seek out and accept available assistance. They recognize the fact that man has but the strength to tease him into self-destructive action and, therefore, they place themselves at the mercy of fate. As they had earlier scanned the shoreline for possible help (from religion as represented by the church and from fellowman as associated with the rescue station), they now humble themselves to accept any assistance—they submit and thereby pay silent homage to an unknown and indifferent force. (106)

This entropic "force," a thrust that adheres these survivors together for the final mad dash at land. The correspondent is reminded of his life-saving escape into art as he gazes ashore: "he was impressed as one who, in a gallery, looks at a scene from Brittany or Algiers" (Crane 142).

---

[1] Norton, Caroline E.S. "Bingen on the Rhine." (Porter and Coates 1883). Norton's long poem tells of a dying soldier's request for word to be sent to his loved ones in the city of his birth, Bingen am Rhein, on Germany's Rhine river.

The correspondent learned that entropy's arm is long, that all systems have little recourse. "Attempts at action lead to inaction—death; but here there is a basis for hope, as death is seen as a state of freedom. Billie achieves this ultimate state—freedom from this earth" (Autrey 109). If Tomkins is correct, one's freedom increases relative to one's "wants" alongside one's "capacities to satisfy them" (*Shame* 36). Constraint results in shame, the state of "being suspended between what [one] wants and what [one] can have" (Frank and Wilson 67). If Crane is indeed "obsessed by death," it may be that Billie gives him an opportunity to exercise freedom, to have death, as it were (Hoffman 55). My hope is that the crew's consciousness-altering experience made not only they the "interpreters" of "the great sea's voice," but all those on the beach, the "men with blankets, clothes, and flasks, and women with coffee-pots and all the remedies sacred to their minds" (144). In these final moments, Billie "knows no subjection of self" (Autrey 103). The communal "welcome of the land to the men from the sea was warm and generous," however, "while Billie's "still and dripping shape," robbed of its energies, serves as the inescapable result of both energy expenditure and individualism (Crane 144).

If Crane's most direct attempt at connecting with the reader is in naming, specifically in giving only Billie the oiler one, why does he "lure the reader into a degree of identification that the anonymity of the other men otherwise stubbornly withholds, only to let the oiler die at the end of the story" (Claviez 149)? Naming, as it happens, is not the only strategy Crane uses to prompt identification. Martin Meisel claims that the reader's experience of the "chaos of battle" in *The Red Badge of Courage* relies on the generality of his main character (263). The novel's protagonist "can scarcely believe his imminent mingling" into the mass of countless soldiers occupying the battlefield (262). Crane's strategy, by way of the protagonist's pseudo-anonymity, is to show the reader battle through an individual point of view but in a way that extends to encompass a broad range of experience:

> [T]he youth's experience of battle is an inseparable amalgam of feeling and perception, fluctuating both in intensity and inwardness. And while nearly all that informs the reader comes through the sensibility of the youth and his purview, it is an enlarged purview rather than a rigid sensory envelope confined to six feet of immediacy … . The language and imagery by which feeling and perception are conveyed also convey the tension between collective

experience and the singularity of a particular consciousness. That tension plays out within the implicit framework that recognizes battles as, simultaneously, an effort to contain chaos and to encourage it. (Meisel 262–63)

For "the member of a cohering collective, the chaos is pushed to the periphery" (263). The sea's chaos parts just enough for the crew to make a final push for the stability of land. Billie perishes alone. His survivalist tendencies are antithetical to the democratic machinery of the crew. The anger he feels at his ineptitude against the sea prohibits him from lasting communion with his crewmates. His tale is cautionary. Crane maintains the remainder of crew's anonymity to discourage additional reader identification. Dissatisfied, readers are receptive to shame, a communal phenomenon, which in the end welcomes us into the fold as "interpreters" of the "great sea's voice" (144). Crane rescues us, too, in the end. If Crane "occupies a position between Whitman's romanticism and of the American self and the modernism of someone like Wallace Stevens," his sails are set toward the latter (Claviez 140).

Works Cited

Autrey, Max L. "The Word out of the Sea: A View of Crane's 'The Open Boat.'" *Arizona Quarterly*, vol. 30, 1974, pp. 101–10.
Claviez, Thomas. "'Declining' the (American) Sublime: Stephen Crane's 'The Open Boat.'" *Amerikastudien/American Studies*, vol. 53, no. 2, 2008, pp. 137–151. JSTOR, www.jstor.org/stable/41158370.
Conder, John J. "The Necessary Fiction." *Naturalism in American Fiction: The Classic Phase*. University Press of Kentucky, 1984, pp. 22–68.
Crane, Stephen. "The Open Boat." *The Oxford Book of Sea Stories*, edited by Tony Tanner. Oxford University Press, 1994, pp. 121–144.
Felksi, Rita. "Identifying with Characters." *Character: Three Inquiries in Literary Studies*. University of Chicago Press, 2019, pp. 77–126.
Gilman, Benjamin Ives. "Art a Tryst." *The Arts*, vol. 6, no. 1, 1924.
Hoffman, Frederick J. "The War and the Postwar Temper." *The Twenties: American Writing in the Postwar Decade*. The Viking Press, 1968, pp. 47–85.
Katz, Joseph. *The Poems of Stephen Crane: A Critical Edition*. Cooper Square Publishing, Inc., 1966.
Keen, Suzanne. *Empathy and the Novel*. Oxford University Press, 2007.
Meisel, Martin. *Chaos Imagined: Literature, Art, Science*. Columbia University Press, 2016.

Moi, Toril. "Rethinking Character." *Character: Three Inquiries in Literary Studies.* University of Chicago Press, 2019, pp. 27–75.

Norton, Caroline E. S. *Bingen on the Rhine*, Porter & Coates, 1883.

Schober, Regina. "'A Problem in Small Boat Navigation': Ocean Metaphors and Emerging Data Epistemology in Stephen Crane's 'The Open Boat' and Jack London's 'The Heathen.'" *Studies in American Naturalism*, vol. 12 no. 1, 2017, p. 70–88. *Project MUSE*, https://doi.org/10.1353/san.2017.0004.

Scruggs, Charles and Lee VanDemarr. *Jean Toomer and the Terrors of American History.* University of Pennsylvania Press, 1998.

Sedgwick, Eve Kosofsky and Adam Frank, editors. *Shame and its Sisters.* Duke University Press, 1995.

Tanner, Tony. "Everything Running Down." *City of Words: American Fiction 1950–1970.* Harper & Row, New York, 1971, pp. 141–52.

———. "Introduction." *The Oxford Book of Sea Stories*, edited by Tony Tanner. Oxford University Press, 1994, pp. xi–xviii.

Tomkins, Silvan. *Shame and it Sisters*, edited by Eve Kosofsky Sedgwick and Adam Frank. Duke University Press, 1995.

Wraith, Matthew. "Throbbing Human Engines: Mechanical Vibration, Entropy and Death in Marinetti, Joyce, Ehrenburg, and Eliot." *Vibratory Modernism*, edited by Anthony Enns and Shelley Trower, Palgrave Macmillan, 2013, pp. 96–114.

CHAPTER 3

Entropic Affect in Jean Toomer's "Withered Skin of Berries"

Abstract In "Withered Skin of Berries," Jean Toomer depicts a setting near stasis, in which the introduction of new information suggests the possibility for increased understanding of a harrowing past. Toomer similarly uses entropic motif to set the stage for a hard-won empathic and epiphanic bonding between Vera and abolitionist John Brown, whose memory haunts the protagonist. As Eliot and Joyce suggest that ancient patterns of meaning making found in, for instance, the ancient Hindu Upanishads and Homer's *Odyssey* remain useful, Toomer shows that recycled fragments of America's squalid history are compatible with his new vision of social adhesion.

Keywords Accumulation • Anger • Disorder • Empathy • Entropy • Equilibrium • Heat death • Shame • Toomer, Jean • "Withered Skin of Berries"

As mentioned above, Jean Toomer's best-known contribution to the Harlem Renaissance, 1923's *Cane*, is his firsthand account of a vanishing spiritual energy within the African American population of the South. Less discussed is the 1922 short story "Withered Skin of Berries," Toomer's

© The Author(s), under exclusive license to Springer Nature Switzerland AG 2025
M. Phillips, *Disorder, Affect, and Modernist Literature*, Palgrave Studies in Affect Theory and Literary Criticism,
https://doi.org/10.1007/978-3-031-92463-7_3

subtle scorning of the human cost of westward expansion.[1] Though *Cane* has dominated the discussion around Toomer up to this point, "Withered Skin of Berries" deserves more recognition as one of a select group of important works published during modernism's annus mirabilis.[2] The short story centers on Vera, a Black woman who can "pass" for white as she lives and works in Washington DC. She divides her free time between three suitors: Carl, David Teyy, and Art Bond. With David, Vera is exposed to realities that awaken her to history's claim on the present as she reorients herself within the world. She experiences physical and social degradation firsthand. The setting is near stasis, in which new information suggests the possibility for increased understanding of a harrowing past. Toomer similarly uses an entropic motif to set the stage for a hard-won empathic and epiphanic bonding between Vera and abolitionist John Brown. As Eliot and Joyce suggest that ancient patterns of meaning making found in, for instance, the ancient Hindu Upanishads and Homer's *Odyssey* remain useful, Toomer shows that recycled fragments of America's squalid history are compatible with his new vision of social adhesion. In a letter to friend and editor Waldo Frank, Toomer discusses the work-in-progress: "As I now vaguely see and feel it, it is tremendous. This whole brown and black world heaving upward against, here and there mixing with the white world. But the mixture being insufficient to absorb the heaving, it but accelerates and fires it" (*Letters* 138). More than a mere story, Toomer considers "Withered" a hypothesis in an ongoing examination of a universe and the behavior of its systems. Openly privileging spiritual over scientific pursuits, Toomer thinks of science as a "system of exact mysteries" ("VII" 435). Even so, he frequently relies on its language and concepts in his writing. The most pervasive concept borrowed from the sciences is entropy, the accumulation of waste ensuant to heat exchange in any system with a fixed quantity of energy. "Withered," for example, depicts a system slowed to dormancy, "pioneer aggressiveness" surrendered "to a southern repose" (139).

Toomer's Washington is already decaying, exposing the underbelly of Vera's ostensibly ordered working world. Vera quarantines herself, both in

---

[1] Foley, in "The Color of Blood John Brown, Jean Toomer, and the New Negro Movement," locates the original publication date of "Withered Skin of Berries" in 1922. *Cane* was published in 1923.

[2] Among these are Virginia Woolf's *Jacob's Room*, T. S. Eliot's "The Waste Land," and James Joyce's *Ulysses*.

"passing" and in abstinence, "a virgin whose notion of purity tape-worms her" (139). The men around try to contaminate her system: "'Vera is a tease.' The thought found its way to her." In a place where "Departmental buildings are grey gastronomic structures" that "suck the life of mediocrities," Vera resists dissolution, a "condiment-like irritability in the process of her digestion." She perseveres variously and with notable flexibility. This way of living is not indefinitely sustainable, however, and her circumstances eventually provoke her to seek connections with others. In Barbara Foley's words, Toomer "aspired to be an apostle of both modernism and social revolution, psychoanalysis and historical materialism" (244). "Withered" demonstrates "the possibilities and the limitations of [his] ambitious aesthetic-cum-political program in the early 1920s" (Foley 244). Toomer, then, seeks to *join*: aesthetics with politics; "narrative realism with lyric symbolism" (Christensen 618). Entropy and its balanced final state, heat death, provide a metaphor apt to capture the considerable scope of his undertaking. The entropic process yields a reordering in which "initial" order "dissolves into a disordered mixture" (Lestienne 119). "Withered" indicates not only this, but also a corollary increase of affect, "here and there mixing."

Disorder typifies both "Withered" and *Cane*. Toomer recounts that *Cane* "'was born in an agony of internal tightness, conflict, and chaos'" (qtd. in Scruggs and VanDemarr 10). It is remarkably turbulent in form and content. Houston Baker deems it a "protest novel, a portrait of the artist, and a thorough delineation of the black situation" (18). Violence and death fill many of its pages, from harrowing scenes of infanticide to mob lynching. Yet in the aftermath of unforgivable tragedy, Toomer attempts to map the way toward an America newly conceived, one that is defined by the dissolution of harmful and outmoded barriers between its peoples. Wanton chaos is reclassified in terms of the entropic *process*, chaos with potential for meaningful transformation. Toomer desires to salvage the complex beauty of the rural South, which fades faster each day in the shadow of industrialization. At the same time, he strives to construct something new. Toomer tests his hypotheses in "Withered." He depicts a Washington, DC that, despite advanced entropic decline, carries the side effect of increased interpersonal understanding. Tomkins outlines the "psychology of commitment" of abolitionists and those they inspire:

> violence and suffering are critical in a democratic society, in heightening antipathy for violations of democratic values and in heightening sympathy

for the victims of such violations. A radical magnification of negative feeling toward the oppressors and of positive feeling toward the oppressed is the major dynamic which powers the commitment first of the individual reformer and then of increasing numbers who are influenced by him. ("Psychology" 270)

Tomkins likewise maintains that a society can rightly be judged on its capacity for fellow feeling. Tomkins's empathy-shame process demands vigilant mindfulness of both one's own inner life and the needs of one's cohabitants: "the fact that the other identities sufficiently with others to be ashamed rather than to show contempt strengthens any social group and its sense of community" (*Shame* 156). Regarding race, Toomer heartily believes in a blending of all ethnicities under the common moniker *American*. His ideal model of race is an amalgamation of many races, "a spiritual fusion analogous to the fact of racial intermingling" ("*Liberator*" 70). "Spiritual fusion" in "Withered" subverts the ostensibly romantic plot and demonstrates how protagonist Vera's isolation abates under the accumulation of both entropy and shame. An empathic bond is consequently fostered joining her and the abolitionist John Brown.

That our universe consists of a network of systems makes its way into Toomer's work: "Since [ours] is a world, not the world, it has boundaries" ("Part" 254). Tomkins views the body in the same way: "I have supposed the person to be a bio-psycho-social entity at the intersect of both more complex higher social systems and lower biological systems" ("Quest" 308). What's more, Tomkins argues that the body is an open (as opposed to closed) system, a sentiment indicated in Toomer in the form of transmissible intolerances: "words," the "germ carries of our prejudices"; "gestures," that of our "antagonisms" ("Germ" 82). To slow the spread, Toomer suggests putting a hold on linguistic accumulation, written and spoken. Alas, this is no panacea: "Seal the mouths of all of us, prohibit writing, destroy all printed matter, and when those who are now infants come of age they would have acquired from us only those antagonisms communicable by gestures." Toomer elsewhere signals unity as cure: "You cannot resolve the problems of separation by operating within the force of separatism" ("Oppose" 111). Hence, Toomer advocates reducing entropic accumulation and denies isolation is of any lasting benefit. This mindset manifests in his fictional worlds, wherein a given environment represents but one of many partitioned worlds. Characters, too, are "systems," all housed within the world-as-text. These characters behave in ways that suggest the permeability, or openness, of systems, as well as the possibility of endurance within even the most entropic among them.

Rita Felski describes the "shock of recognition" one might undergo by way of character identification—an experience that prompts the dismantling of the self and, subsequently, a reorganizing of the self in an upgraded form (81). One may *identify* with fictional characters behaving empathically and through them *connect* empathically with those actual persons around them. An inversion of this phenomenon manifests in "Withered." John Brown is represented in the story as a "body" that routinely "rumbles in the river" and "thunders down the falls" (148). In Toomer's Washington, Brown is less player than presence. To Vera, Brown is a fiction, as it were. This ontological mise en abyme allows for an inversion of identification: Vera fails to meaningfully identify with the men with whom she interacts, but, through them, empathizes with John Brown.

The men in Vera's life bring her contrasting degrees of excitement, in Tomkins's sense of the word. Tomkins privileges the interest-exciting affect highly amongst positive affects.[3] "'I am, above all, what excites me,'" Tomkins says (qtd in. Frank and Wilson 54). Carl, Vera's white coworker is socially and morally inert. The two share a symbiotic relationship. She feeds on Carl's torpor, the "inward anemia of Vera fed on [Carl] … . She established a sort of moral equilibrium and dulled a growing sense of deceit by resolving not to tease him" (140). A life with Carl is synonymous with predictability, boredom. Vera tolerates Carl's company at work, but he does not excite her. In fact, after an "unexpected" day off leaves her no excuse to keep Carl at bay, Vera feels "herself getting hot, as if her nerves were heated pins and needles pricking her." Overexposed to Carl, Vera experiences the effects of anger due to "Cognitive hypersimplicty" and the "narrowing of the cognitive field" (*Shame* 206). Repetition experienced subjectively—in this case, spending too much time with humdrum Carl—builds up to anger, which fuels the other affects. Angry, Vera's excitement is amplified such that she intuits significance in her surroundings: "Negroes were working on the basin of an artificial lake that was to spread its smooth glass surface before Lincoln's Memorial. The shadow of their emancipator stirred them neither to bitterness or awe. The scene was a photograph on Vera's eye-balls" (141). Vera romanticizes this spectacle,

---

[3] We can think of interest-excitement as "'a support of the necessary and the possible,' as 'a necessary condition for the formation of the perceptual world' and in creative experiences of all kinds" (Frank and Wilson 52–53).

feeling "an unprecedented nostalgia, a promise of awakening." However, her misplaced reminiscence for the initial order combined with an "insufficient interest" in the men and "their emancipator" stifles any potential identification or empathy.

In addition to Carl, there is David, who has been characterized as both "a black man who symbolizes … the energy of a new African-American consciousness" (Scruggs and VanDemarr 162) and "a middle-class would-be liberated artist, who also displays sexist tendencies" (Kukrechtová 140). I concur with Siobhan B. Somerville's claim that David "serves as a catalyst for the events of the story; his presence serves to expose the other characters' unpredictable and unconventional desires, manifested simultaneously in cross-racial and same-sex attraction" (Somerville 149). Undoubtedly, David is an energy source, and his poetry excites Vera; and, like her, he is isolated, "closed up in himself" (Toomer, "Withered" 141).[4] Vera's recollection of his verse motivates her to blurt out words she'd "'never said before'" (142). Vera cathects with David, and his memory provokes an "uncertain attempt at recapturing [the] mood which … was new and strange to her" (143). Vera fails to acquire her object of excitement; hence, this "mood lay fallow" (143). The shame affect is closely associated with interest-excitement. Shame is elicited when "barriers" debar one from "objects of excitement and enjoyment" (*Shame* 150). Therefore, Vera is subject to shame at the failed acquisition of her object of excitement.

"John Brown's body," figuratively floats along the river, the "brown burden of a wasted sediment" (143). A Connecticut-born abolitionist, Brown historically stood for persistence and progress. According to Foley, "Vera views the river's 'brown sediment'—and, by extension, herself, or at least her 'brown' ancestry—as something 'wasted,' a 'burden,' the dross left at the bottom of the melting pot" (247). Vera, in time, sees that the "landscape she beholds is not just a geographical site, but a historical process. The continuing material reality of John Brown—his body—has been carried down the violent river of U. S. history and mingled with the rising and falling tides of the modern world" (Foley 248). Brown's body symbolizes a perseverance and fortitude that allow his memory to persist and blend significantly into the present. Vera's eventual recognition of Brown reveals the importance of what she has heretofore "repressed" (Foley 247). Toomer's interpretation of Brown's stalwart antiracism stands in

---

[4] Hereafter cited "Withered."

opposition to the overwhelming entropic degeneration that has left Washington faceless and grey. His works "testify to the abiding influence of New Negro postwar radicalism, as well as to its figuration of John Brown as symbol of uncompromising antiracist militancy" (Foley 243). For Vera, Brown's memory translates into the more immediate desire for interpersonal connection, however short-lived, within a degenerating system.

Vera's suitors represent varying degrees of predictability, both in their compliance with industrialism and perpetuation of racial biases and prejudice. Carl is fully assimilated into the industrial world, "quite happily absorbed in the handling of his car" ("Withered" 143). His social standpoint is decidedly racist, and his view of America in general is jaded. Carl's postwar America "don't give a young fellow with push and brains and energy half a chance." Carl rejects the fact that energy in his system is finite, insisting that action and energy are what "America stands for." Incorporated into industrial America, he rejects any meaningful connection to others, contending that the "spirit of the country is one of individual enterprise." Carl bleakly assesses the nation's trajectory, declaring that the "Argentine is virginal." He is erroneously hoping Vera can help him learn Spanish, so he can one day "clean up" in South America. "I was born in America, just like you," says Vera, "English is the only language that I know" (144). Vera reflects Toomer's concept of a people "naturally and inevitably" American ("*Liberator*" 70). This is how he saw himself: one with a diverse background who becomes simply American in the present democratic age. Carl conversely rejects the empathy characteristic of a democracy, instead reveling in a sense of self-importance garnered from lands he foolishly aspires to conquer.

Vera and Carl's differences are irreconcilable, not least because Carl rejects a progressive democratic landscape that necessitates the fruitful merging of people with diverse ethnic backgrounds. This joining depends on the tearing down of outmoded social barriers, those Carl reinforces by clinging to white supremacy. The rift between them widens, illustrated by the divergence of their physical appearance. Dusk's "violet" light causes Carl to mirror the "scant foliage of clustered trees," contrasting with Vera's "purple" glow ("Withered" 145). Vera is distracted by the vague memory of David. Carl believes his connection with Vera is growing, but meaningful connection between them is impossible: "Carl wholeheartedly embraces the doctrines of racial supremacy, male superiority, and imperialist domination" (Foley 245). These major barriers keep him closed off from Vera. Since Carl is stagnant, closed off to new viewpoints and experiences, his system remains dominated by the initial order anathema to the new disordered mixture. Having cathected with David, Vera dreads returning to the Carl's grey, mechanical world. David "has taken something from me. It will be harder to face the office" ("Withered" 147). Carl's flatness is complicated by his past exchanges with David. Carl believes he experienced something akin to empathy when he and David were college students: "I think I began to feel like he did." Carl recounts David's pontification:

> Dead leaves of northern Europe, Carl, have decayed for roots tangled here in America. Roots thrusting up a stark fresh life. That's you. Multi-colored leaves, tropics, temperate, have decayed for me. We meet here where a race has died for both of us. Only a few years ago, forests and fields, this lake, Mendota, heard the corn and hunting songs of a vanished people. They have resolved their individualism to a common stream. We live on it. We live on them. And we are growing. Life lives on itself and grows.

While not glorifying the nation's colonial history, David does point out how colonization paved the way for two of them to be together in that moment. Destruction resulted in an equilibrium of sorts, a "common stream." Carl "yearns to be immersed in the 'common stream' conjoining African American and Indian cultures" (Foley 245). But his biases and prejudices keep him from any meaningful identification with the Indigenous people in David's story; therefore, an empathic connection with David is impossible.

On the other hand, in uttering for the first time his own story, Carl can—through Vera—identify with the "repressed" version of himself. He recounts to her what he considers sensitive details of his past with David: "'He closed his hand over mine. Me, a football man, holding hands with a man on the lake. If that had ever got out it would have done for me. But it never did. I could never tell it. Only to you. You are the first" ("Withered" 147–48). Peter Christensen contends that "If Carl loves Vera, then when he says … 'I felt like this,' we know that he must have been in love with David Teyy also" (619). Carl ultimately uses Vera as the vessel through which to relive this "perfect homoerotic moment" (Christensen 619). Carl fails to identify with Vera. Nonetheless, by objectifying her—mentally transforming her into a fictional version of himself—he empathizes through her, thus reliving the experience with David, although we know that Carl's disposition would keep him from fully admitting this to himself. Somerville attests that "Carl's chagrin ... and his shame ... signal that Carl self-consciously acknowledges the implications of this homoerotic moment. He is clearly admitting his capacity to feel sexual desire for another man, which does not necessarily preclude his desire for women, but also registers his fear that his reputation might be damaged if he were labeled a 'homosexual'" (147). Toomer shows that the potential bond between Carl and David was thwarted by Carl's stalwart adherence to obsolescent ideals. Toomer therefore censures the dominant conceptions of the American male, revealing that a fear of breaking down barriers results in lifelong stagnation.

Vera later prompts Art to share a story of his own. Art appears to have experienced authentic empathy, if only for a moment. Art tells the story of the cane-boiling "syrup-man":

> I saw my body there, seated with the other men. As I looked, it seemed to dissolve, and melt with the others that were dissolving too. They were a stream. They flowed up-stream from Africa and way up to a height where the light was so bright I could hardly see, burst into a multi-colored spraying fountain. My throat got tight. I guess it was that that pulled me back into myself[.] ("Withered" 151)

This one scene has received perhaps the most attention of any moment in this underresearched story. As Catherine Keyser observes, "In the very sugar cane that provided the raw material for the industry that mobilized the transatlantic slave trade ... Toomer found an unexpected model for formal metamorphosis ... . Toomer depicts sugar cane as a substance that shifts states and alters consciousness ... . [T]he shifting states of cane could represent dissolving boundaries between races and bodies" (285–86). The powerful "substance" provides one explanation. "This ejaculatory vision of the multi-colored diaspora," writes Keyser, "connects the chemical properties of a dissolving substance with the hallucinatory possibility of transcending self and forging community" (286). For Somerville, the "syrup-man" scene not only recalls Carl's admission to Vera, but also blurs the story's color lines:

> Although it is more metaphoric than Carl's encounter with David Teyy on the boat, Art's dream is clearly homoerotic, with its orgasmic imagery and language of 'dissolving' and 'melting' with other men. The desire that Art

describes, however, depends as much on racial identification and (perhaps interracial) mingling as it does on homoeroticism. The 'stream' begins in Africa and, through its blending with other men, becomes a 'multi-colored spraying fountain.' This description also ties Art's dream to the figure of David Teyy, who is referred to as the 'man of the multi-colored leaves.' (148)

It is likely that Art was able to connect with the men because his "mingling" was motivated by "racial identification" and not solely "homoeroticism." This is reasonable considering that David "is the erotic center of this story, the figure who mediates sexual desire for all the characters" (Somerville 149). I have argued elsewhere that in "Kabnis," the final part of *Cane*, Toomer explores an array of possible candidates for his ideal American (Phillips 220). None of these characters wins out definitively; instead, we join Toomer on an exploratory journey through their thoughts and actions, as he attempts to sketch out an exemplar. He uses a similar strategy in "Withered" in the form of Vera's three suitors, none of which have offered her truly meaningful identification. Nevertheless, David does have a special claim on Vera's thoughts; regardless of whose company she keeps, Vera remains preoccupied with David.

Without a doubt, Art only brings Vera closer to David. Art acts as conduit between Vera and David. The disapproving flora pulls her from his grasp: "Trees stand still, glowering, in a stationary sky … . Weeds tangled in her uncurled hair" ("Withered" 152). Even Art's passive utility is botched once he tries to force himself on Vera, and her cutting words "return him to slavery" (Foley 245). Art and Brown merge in Vera's mind: "she heard [Art] splashing through the creek … [John Brown's body] thunders down the falls." As if warding off her own merging, she "buried her teeth in the ground to steady the convulsions of her sobbing." This shameful experience motivates Vera to cut herself off and seal herself in, to seek claustral sanctuary. She buries herself in her work. Tomkins argues that attempts to envelop oneself in this way harken back to our "earliest modes of togetherness … one inside of the other, in the womb, in the arms, in the mouth" (*Shame* 89). Vera's temporary escape is interrupted by her growing distaste for the job, a reflection of Toomer's condemnation of the industrial world. Foley claims that Toomer "viewed the negation of capitalism as essential to the achievement of racial equality" (243), and we see from the outset of the story Toomer's caricature of post-industrialism. The story reveals a critique of racism, industrialism, and the difficulty of progress in a world that perpetuates both. Vera struggles to convince herself that the repetitive working world is where she belongs. She occupies an interstitial place, a "curious haze" ("Withered" 152). Vera's failure to cloister indeterminately inside the gray machine world is confirmed when her coworkers reveal their prejudices upon discovering another woman "passing": "The way they boast about progress and all that youd [*sic*] think theyd [*sic*] be satisfied with their own race. But theyre [*sic*] not, theyre [*sic*] always trying to push into ours" (154). The monotony of the industrial world combined with the sobering reminder of society's endless prejudice results in anger, the "hot affect" (*Shame* 197), dramatized when Vera "plunged into a hot bath and tried to vaporize herself, one with its fumes" ("Withered" 155). Her desire for total dissolution made clear, she prepares to meet David, experiencing the "sincere impression that for the first time in her life she was really beautiful."

Foley claims that David is a "projection of Toomer's idealized vision of himself—who challenges [Vera] to overcome her knotted internal state" (244). David's language echoes that of thermodynamics: "The necessary complement of giving is the capacity to take" ("Withered" 156). Vera does not find solace in her work, but she does with David, "as if she was in the dark enclosure of a womb" (155). Vera's anger having been previously activated, she now harbors the capacity for energy transfer. Though it will inevitably create more waste energy in the system, this type of exchange results also in useful heat. David says the following to Vera: "Life is inconceivable except in relation to its surrounding forms … . The process and mystery of life. Life feeding on itself." Here, Toomer reveals how energy behaves in the system of his text. Life must feed on itself to continue. This is how individual systems persist under entropic decline. Entropy builds, but the system must go on until heat death. Toomer illustrates this process: "souls drifting to the rhythm of forgotten cadences, whirled up … and growing" (156). The remnants of life feeding on itself, unusable waste energy, forgotten, but still implicated in the processes of the past and bearing its memory. David explains how progress is essential to life's process, how "Things die. Transmute. Their memory lingers" (157). As in *Cane*, Toomer does not fully reject the nation's past, its problematic history and complex beauty. We come to see that he may see himself in David, but he likewise sees himself in Vera. Vera is ready to move into the next phase, to "plunge in the river" and "cross over into camp ground" (157).

Vera's failure to identify with her three suitors leaves her primed for an empathic communion with John Brown. A role reversal occurs. Instead of being accused, Vera accuses David: "you whom I turn to, tease me. Whom I love. Who carry solution within you. Who could, but by a touch, make me feel the world not so . . . utterly outside, and me alone" (158). David knows that what Vera needs does not come from an outside source: "Perfect within yourself, incarnate mystery" (158). Vera believes she suffers a "shameful defect," making her incapable of meaningful communion (148). In actuality, shame is dependent on positive affects. Toomer infuses his story with numerous references to America's history of racism, slavery, and colonization. On "Conduit Road," history represented "Across the river" by the archaeological site at the "Potomac palisades," John Brown's body follows Vera and David (159). At this historical nexus, Vera undergoes an inverse identification: "Shook with a strange convulsion. . . . Something so complete and overpowering came over her that she sank, almost senseless, to her knees" (159). Vera undergoes a shock of recognition by virtue of her failed identification with David, thus connecting empathically with John Brown. Vera realizes her attraction to David is really an attraction to what she sees in him: "A burning integrity of vision" (160). Such integrity Vera has already shown. She has always existed apart, a whole unto herself. This is what Toomer seeks to show us: the very entropic circumstances that resulted in Vera's detachment from her surroundings ultimately allow for her crucial empathic communion with the one who shared a similar burning integrity of vision. Toomer challenges the significance of empathy in the following pages: "The western world demands of us that we not escape. The implication of fresh life is its use" (162). The story concludes by repeating its previous sections, suggesting a closed system. Vera ultimately experiences an empathic communion with Brown that could deepen her connection with the heritage that she must hide. If this leads to shame, "shame is an experience of the self by the self"; it will only enhance her self-awareness (*Shame* 136). "In a democratic society," writes Tomkins, "contempt will often be replaced by empathic shame, in which the critic hangs his head in shame at what the other has done" (139). Even in contempt, there lies potential for Vera's experience to multiply, for "the same psychological dynamic underlies the commitment of the individual and the group" ("Psychology" 270).

Works Cited

Baker, Jr., Houston A. "Journey toward Black Art: Jean Toomer's *Cane*." *Afro-American Poetics: Revisions of Harlem and the Black Aesthetic*. University of Wisconsin Press, 1988, pp. 11–44.

Christensen, Peter. "Sexuality and Liberation in Jean Toomer's 'Withered Skin of Berries.'" *Callaloo*, no. 36, 1988, pp. 616–626. *JSTOR*, www.jstor.org/stable/2931546.

Felksi, Rita. "Identifying with Characters." *Character: Three Inquiries in Literary Studies*. University of Chicago Press, 2019, pp. 77–126.

Foley, Barbara. "The Color of Blood: John Brown, Jean Toomer, and the New Negro Movement." *African American Review*, vol. 46, no. 2–3, 2013, pp. 237–253. *EBSCOhost*, http://search.ebscohost.com/login.aspx?direct=true&db=mzh&AN=2014383306&site=ehost-live.

Keyser, Catherine. "Bottles, Bubbles, and Blood: Jean Toomer and the Limits of Racial Epidermalism." *Modernism/Modernity*, vol. 22, no. 2, 2015, pp. 279–302. *ProQuest*, https://login.libproxy.uncg.edu/login?url=https://www.proquest.com/scholarly-journals/bottles-bubbles-blood-jean-toomer-limits-racial/docview/1707489813/se-2.

Kukrechtová, Daniela. "'Remove the [Red] Tape' of Respectability: Jazzy Transformations in Jean Toomer's Washington, D.C." *CEA Critic*, vol. 81, no. 2, 2019, pp. 130–152. *ProQuest*, https://login.libproxy.uncg.edu/login?url=https://www.proquest.com/scholarly-journals/remove-red-tape-respectability-jazzy/docview/2267372500/se-2.

Lestienne, Remy. "The Age of Things, Order and Chaos, Entropy and Information." *The Children of Time: Causality, Entropy, Becoming*. Translated by E. C. Neher. University of Illinois Press, 1995, pp. 119.

Phillips, Matt. "Entropy and Equilibrium in Jean Toomer's *Cane*." *Mississippi Quarterly*, vol. 74 no. 2, 2021, p. 203–225. *Project MUSE*, https://doi.org/10.1353/mss.2022.0004.

Scruggs, Charles and Lee VanDemarr. *Jean Toomer and the Terrors of American History*. University of Pennsylvania Press, 1998.

Somerville, Siobhan B. *Queering the Color Line: Race and the Invention of Homosexuality in American Culture*, Duke University Press, 2000. *ProQuest Ebook Central*, https://ebookcentral-proquest-com.libproxy.uncg.edu/lib/uncg/detail.action?docID=3007878.

Tomkins, Silvan. *Shame and it Sisters*. Duke University Press, 1995.

———. "The Psychology of Commitment: The Constructive Role of Violence and Suffering for the Individual and for His Society." *The Antislavery Vanguard: New Essays on the Abolitionists*, edited by Martin Duberman. Princeton University Press, 1965, pp. 270–98.

Tomkins, Silvan. "The Quest for Primary Motives: Biography and Autobiography of an Idea." *Journal of Personality and Social Psychology*, vol. 41, no. 2, 1981, pp. 306–29.

Toomer, Jean. "Germ Carriers." *A Jean Toomer Reader*, edited by Frederick L. Rusch Oxford University Press, 1993a, pp. 82.

———. "Oppose the Force, Not the Man." *A Jean Toomer Reader*, edited by Frederick L. Rusch Oxford University Press, 1993b, pp. 110–11.

———. "Part of a Universe." *A Jean Toomer Reader*, edited by Frederick L. Rusch Oxford University Press, 1993c, pp. 253–57.

———. *The Letters of Jean Toomer, 1919–1924*, edited by Mark Whalan. University of Tennessee Press, 2006a.

———. "To the Liberator." 19 August 1922. Letter 51 of *The Letters of Jean Toomer, 1919–1924*, edited by Mark Whalan. University of Tennessee Press, 2006b, pp. 70–71.

———. "VII: Indications." *The Wayward and the Seeking*, edited by Darwin T. Turner. Howard University Press, 1980a, pp. 435.

———. "Withered Skin of Berries." *The Wayward and the Seeking*, edited by Darwin T. Turner. Howard University Press, 1980b, pp. 139–65.

CHAPTER 4

Necessary Entropy in Virginia Woolf's *To the Lighthouse*

Abstract The memory of Virginia Woolf's mother permeates her 1927 family-focused novel, *To the Lighthouse*. Woolf's novel provides a thorough and personal picture of the weight of accumulating entropy through the gradual unraveling of the Ramsay family alongside Lily Briscoe, a painter working on a fitting memento of their shared coastal sojourns. Mr. and Mrs. Ramsay's opposing approaches to decline show equally opposing outcomes. The novel reveals a process of renovation akin to Tomkins's conception of a "strong theory," wherein Lily's final brushstroke and the remarkable interpersonal connections in the novel's latter pages anticipate the end of the accumulative process.

Keywords Accumulation • Disorder • Equilibrium • Empathy • Entropy • Heat death • Renovation • Strong Theory • *To the Lighthouse* • Work • Woolf, Virginia

The Ramsays's Hebrides summer home off the coast of Scotland is the setting for one of Virginia Woolf's most celebrated novels, 1927's *To the Lighthouse*. Woolf's narrative displays the gradual unraveling of the Ramsay family alongside a handful of friendly acquaintances, including Lily Briscoe, a painter working on a fitting memento of the shared coastal sojourns.

© The Author(s), under exclusive license to Springer Nature
Switzerland AG 2025
M. Phillips, *Disorder, Affect, and Modernist Literature*, Palgrave Studies in Affect Theory and Literary Criticism,
https://doi.org/10.1007/978-3-031-92463-7_4

Graham Fraser postulates that the dwelling is "very much a Victorian, nineteenth-century home. Reading its fall into ruin as an architectural metaphor for the abandonment of an untenable, nineteenth-century aesthetic at the dawn of the Modernist era opens the way to read its ruin as a case study in renovation—a modernist 'making it new'—that, paradoxically, requires the old to fall into disrepair" (119). Considering this, renovation is akin to entropy inasmuch as production follows destruction. I reiterate Tomkins's remarks that a "strong theory" forms "through endless processes of construction, destruction, and reconstruction." If renovation is the mutual object of these like phenomena, then their modus operandi is accumulation: they manifest as sums.

These phenomena also influence coterminous systems. Hatfield et al. discuss "emotional contagion," how people respond physically to others' emotional output: "As people nonconsciously and automatically mimic their companions' fleeting expressions of emotion, they often come to feel pale reflections of their partners' feelings. By attending to this stream of tiny moment-to-moment reactions, people can and do 'feel themselves into' the emotional landscape inhabited by their partners" (96). Keeping to Lakoff and Johnson's coining of the "container metaphor," it is helpful to imagine *To the Lighthouse* as a system. Said differently, Woolf's novels are "self-manifesting; they constitute a total universe and sustain themselves within the completeness of their own vision" (Fletcher and Bradbury 409). Woolf's "hive" description supplies an image that calls to mind Tomkins's body-as-system model:

> How then ... did one know one thing or another thing about people, sealed as they were? Only like a bee, drawn by some sweetness of sharpness in the air intangible to touch or taste, one haunted the dome-shaped hive, ranged the wastes of the air over the countries of the world alone, and then haunted the hives with their murmurs and their stirring; the hives, which were people. (51)

A system as such, *To the Lighthouse* accepts the laws of thermodynamics, and Woolf's handling of entropy and its influence shows both its inevitability and its necessity. I repeat the notion that constant energy exchanges degrade all matter within a closed system until heat death/equilibrium. *To the Lighthouse* illustrates this process when the partitions that circumscribe the "hive" capitulate to accumulation. Woolf's entropic portrait of the Ramsays shows decay giving rise to creation through a process of renovation.

Woolf's representation of entropy is fitting for her era, given the monumental advancements in industry and the harrowing realities of the Great War pressing on people's minds:

> Initially, the emphasis is on fragmentation, on the breaking up and the progressive disintegration of those meticulously constructed 'systems' and 'types' and 'absolutes' that lived on from the earlier years of the century, on the destruction of the belief in large general laws to which all life and conduct could be claimed to be subject. As a second stage … there came a restructuring of parts, a re-relating of the fragmented concepts, a re-ordering of linguistic entities to match what was felt to be the new order of reality … . Finally, in its ultimate stages, thought seemed to undergo something analogous to a change of state: a dissolving, a blending, a merging of things previously held to be forever mutually exclusive. (McFarlane 80)

Much of *To the Lighthouse* is characterized by an intricate power struggle between Mrs. and Mr. Ramsay that mirrors this transition from fragmentation to blending. Mrs. Ramsay's range of influence is vast, challenged only by her husband, who wields comparable energies. Mrs. Ramsay endeavors to keep Mr. Ramsay's entropic influence in check, a form of protection for the children. Paul Tolliver Brown observes that she "manages to maintain her own traditional position as the force that binds, in spite of her husband … . Although Mr. Ramsay's separateness is an antithetical force to Mrs. Ramsay's connectedness, Mrs. Ramsay loves her husband all the more for the very step-by-step, cause and effect reassurance that his presence confers" (43). Mr. Ramsay threatens the sanctuary his wife creates around the children. Still, she values the sense of order that her husband provides, one of the "fabric of tradition she so prizes, including the ideas of opposing gender roles and their unity in marriage" (Brown 43).

Orderly on the surface, Mr. Ramsay is the truthfully the emblem of disorder: "Every time he approached … ruin approached, chaos approached" (Woolf 148). Indeed, the entropic Mr. Ramsay makes possible the blurring of identities between the Ramsays and the Sorleys who await them at the Lighthouse. Woolf indicates this merging of personalities early in the novel, when small son James acts as "measuring block for the Lighthouse keeper's little boy" (26). Mrs. Ramsay will in fact contribute to the accumulation of waste responsible for the Sorleys's degraded environment with her gifts: the "reddish-brown stocking she was knitting," alongside "a pile of old magazines, and some tobacco, indeed, whatever she could find lying about, not really wanted, but only littering the room, to give those poor fellows, who must be bored to death sitting all day with nothing to do" (5). A kind if condescending gesture, and a misguided one. Her offering of what ultimately amounts to waste hastens the degeneration of the Sorleys's environment. Adding entropy deepens the "grey-green somnolence which embraced them all" (10).

Mrs. Ramsay's gift is anathema for one preoccupied with difference. She condemns anyone who "invent[s] differences" when people are "different enough" (8). Some difference she considers "real," class and status markers such as "rich and poor, high and low" (9). Real difference is inseparable from the individual; in the "birth" and "blood" of a person resides the basis of the "social problem" she finds "Insoluble" (9). Insoluble indeed, given her keen awareness of the work required to maintain her own children's safety and the Ramsays' way of life. Shuddering to think what it would take to maintain outsized compromise, Mrs. Ramsay is more comfortable pondering difference from a distance: the "hoary Lighthouse, distant, austere," rescues her from thoughts of "working men" (12). The Sorleys's plight, in particular, is more tolerable viewed from far away. Still, Mrs. Ramsay tends to influence the emotional self-preservation of those closest to her. When Mr. Ramsay dispels any notion of a Lighthouse trip, Mrs. Ramsay soothes James, sentry against father's "caustic" words (15). This family dynamic leaves Mrs. Ramsay wavering between her love for her husband and her fear of his influence on the children. This unsteady state parallels the aftermath of the era's immense social and cultural transformation: "A sense of flux, the notion of continuum, the running together of things in ways often contrary to the dictates of simple common sense (though familiar enough in dream) alone seemed able to help in the understanding of certain bewildering and otherwise inexplicable phenomena of contemporary life" (McFarlane 80–81).

Lily Briscoe, on the other hand, is mostly unrestrained by the emotional ties that weigh down the Ramsays. She is primarily driven by her need to capture and fortify them on her canvas. Benjamin Ives Gilman explains that the creation of art requires the artist to enter a distinctive emotional space separate from themselves. Sure, Lily is not completely out of harm's way, as when Mr. Ramsay threatens her painting: "he almost knocked her easel over, coming down upon her with his hands waving shouting out" (Woolf 17). But Mr. Ramsay is somewhat innocuous, both "ridiculous" and "alarming." But as long as he keeps moving, expending his own energy, Lily can continue to create; as long as he "would not stand still and look at her picture." Woolf creates a situation where Lily can repurpose Mr. Ramsay's expended energy from a safe distance. The work of art is born out of a place of "ecstasy," or stasis (Gilman 15). In an aesthetics where stasis makes way for art, increased opportunities for stasis correlate with increased opportunities for artistic creation. Mrs. Ramsay's energies have created a sort of equilibrium on the island, and Lily enterprises to place this scene amongst "distant views [which] seem to outlast by a million years (Lily thought) the gazer and to be communing already with a sky which beholds an earth entirely at rest" (Woolf 20). Lily intends to capture and repurpose this scene into a remote and ceaseless wellspring of artistic inspiration.

Woolf casts Lily and Mr. Ramsay in opposition. Lily repurposes the chaos in Mr. Ramsay's wake such that some useful renovation manifests. Mr. Ramsay's "waving" and "shouting," the useless expenditure of energy that brings the island closer to heat death: "It suddenly gets cold. The sun seems to give less heat" (19). But Lily can capture the meaning made on the island in a permanent state on her canvas. Though the Ramsays sail toward heat death, "creative energy," as J. Hillis Miller puts it, still exists (169). One key tension in Woolf is this:

> the question of whether there is beneath the manifold human activities of doing, thinking, talking, writing, creating a rhythmical groundswell which is comforting and sustaining; or whether such rhythm as there is outside human constructing beats out no more than the measure of approaching death. To go on talking, thinking, doing writing, creating is either a way of warding off the fall, ... or if there is somewhere support ... to rest in ... the secret rhythm of creation. (Miller 168)

The elephant in the room is that the "goal Mrs. Ramsay reaches in the novel [indeed] is death" (Miller 170). Her attempts to maintain the divisions that, for her, scaffold regular family life ultimately fail. On top of this, her death mirrors the "vanishing in the catastrophe of the Great War of all that Victorian and Edwardian world of assured social order" (Miller 170). But what of those who survive Mrs. Ramsay? Is it by accident or luck that Mr. Ramsay outlives his wife and son and daughter? If sidestepping entropy as Lily does results in moments of increased creativity, would not the increase of expended energy only add to entropy's accumulation? After all, Mr. Ramsay is responsible for the bulk of accumulation, which results in not only his survival, but also the merging he and James share with the Lighthouse keeper and his ailing son.

Guest of honor William Bankes accuses the Ramsay patriarch of burning out early, of being "one of those men who do their best work before they are forty" (Woolf 23). This entropic description of Mr. Ramsay inspires in Lily's mind "accumulated impressions ... poured in a ponderous avalanche" (24). The "intensity of her perception" incites an objective analysis of interpersonal feeling: "How did one judge people, think of them? How did one add up this and that and conclude that it was liking one felt, or disliking?" (24). This emotional accumulation leaves Lily "transfixed," along with her surroundings, "for eternity." She remembers that "scrubbed kitchen table, symbol of her profound respect for Mr. Ramsay's mind." Finally, the scene "exploded of its own intensity; she felt released." Woolf suggests a meaningful exchange occurs, as Lily" stepped through the gap ... straight into Mr. Ramsay" (25). Anthony Cuda writes that the "figure" of "opening and closing" doors "is one of the ways that Woolf allegorizes those sudden movements when we are exposed to the harshness and violence of the 'not ourselves'" (148). Mr. Ramsay's symbolic slamming of the door reiterates his penchant for isolation.

Fittingly, Mr. Ramsay attempts to escape into a subsystem of his own. After Lily threatens his solitude, we see him perform a "curious gathering together of his person, as if he wrapped himself about and needed privacy into which to regain his equilibrium" (30–31). We also glimpse his wife's capacity for emotional exchange, stimulated by her husband's concurrent entropic outburst and, significantly, tied to thoughts of art: "She stroked James's head; she transferred to him what she felt for her husband, and ... thought what a delight it would be to her should he turn out a great artist" (31). Woolf grants Mrs. Ramsay a remarkable ability to bear her husband's intense emotional brunt, key for maintaining order in her husband's wake. Mrs. Ramsay struggles to keep her husband isolated from the rest of the system, becoming in the process a "sponge sopped full of human emotions" (32). Despite his prowess at avoiding intimacy, her husband acknowledges that he must relinquish isolation, must "step over" and intermingle with those from whom he has deliberately withdrawn. Mr. Ramsay allows for only brief moments of feeling, short breaks in his march toward maximum disorder. His return to the comfort and familiarity of repetition is marked by his mantra, "Some one had blundered" (33). However, we observe Mr. Ramsay undergoing a transformation: "his note ... changed," portending a "new mood" (34). He anticipates equilibrium: he "looked once at his wife and son in the window, and ... without his distinguishing either his son or his wife, the sight of them fortified him and satisfied him and consecrated his effort to arrive at a perfectly clear understanding of the problem which now engaged the energies of his splendid mind" (33).

The "problem" is Mr. Ramsay's well-studied intellectual stalemate, his "sense of failure [which] results from his unsuccessful attempt to reach all the way to Z in his philosophical thinking" (Brown 169). All systems, after a period of peak intensity, and because of this intensity, are likewise extinguished by overwhelming waste energy. Mr. Ramsay stalled intellectual pursuits no longer successfully distracting him from his emotions. He "requires" the self-centered exchange of "sympathy"; not to share in experience, but to "tell the story of his suffering" (Woolf 36). James detests his father's selfish emotional needs, instead opting for his mother's steady "attention" which beams outward (37). James resents that his father threatens the stability of the environment: his "emotion ... vibrating round them, disturbed the perfect simplicity and good sense of his relations with his mother" (36–37). Justin Sausman observes that the "contrast between vibration and stillness emphasizes the gap between life and fiction" in Woolf (45). Mr. Ramsay's emotional "trembling" seems disingenuous when compared to James's relationship with his mother. Mr. Ramsay wants to be "taken within the circle of life, warmed and soothed" (Woolf 37). His is a misguided desire, for "It was sympathy he wanted, to be assured of his genius." He rejects an intimate bond with those who dwell with him there in the "heart of life" for adoration from strangers "all over the world." Unsatisfied, the "fatal sterility of the male plunged itself" into his wife's emotional sphere. Mrs. Ramsay reassures him: "it was real; the house was full; the garden blowing" (38). This exchange leaves Mr. Ramsay "restored [and] renewed" but depletes his wife such that "there was scarcely a shell of herself left for her to know herself by." Out of this destruction, as she "seemed to fold herself together ... and the whole fabric fell in exhaustion upon itself," we see a new "successful creation," her ability "to enclose her and her husband ... as they combine" (38–39).

Such renovation constitutes a net positive, leaving Mrs. Ramsay "finer than her husband"; nevertheless, she is "discomposed," knowing that their union is sustained on half-truths about her husband's social standing and the securities the Ramsays enjoy (39). The "simplicity" of her magnanimity is called into question: perhaps "all this desire of hers to give, to help, was vanity" (41). Her husband, too, shows insecurity, lamenting his intellectual aspirations. Undistracted by enthusiastic and auspicious truth-seeking, he is left to meditate on the creative potential of the unexceptional individual: "He would argue that the world exists for the average human being; that the arts are merely a decoration imposed on the top of human life" (43). Despite this empathic moment, Mr. Ramsay remains dissatisfied with his accomplishments, preoccupied with the elusive "thing he might have done" (45).

Woolf uses Lily's detached perspective to expose Mr. Ramsay's "disguise" and reveal that he is "venerable and laughable at one and the same time" (45). Lily ponders the same issues as the Ramsays, the "divisions" that separate, yet she is at peace with the necessary unification: "If you are exalted you must somehow come a cropper" (45). Lily envisions a scene of all things becoming equal akin to heat death. She observes this phenomenon between the Ramsays: the "love" that is "meant to be spread over the world and become part of the human gain" (47). Lily contemplates "little separate incidents" collecting into a "whole like a wave." This process, this "rapture," is itself an accumulation, with the "same effect as the solution of a scientific problem" that leaves "chaos subdued." Thus, the abstract concept of "love" manifests as an observable process, as in the "digestive system of plants." An apt analogy for renovation: food is taken in, broken down, absorbed as nutrients, the waste done away with.

This is not to say that Lily disrespects Mr. Ramsay entirely; her view of the Ramsays is complex. Above all, Lily admires Mrs. Ramsay's ability to contain (her husband's) chaos, and this is why Lily studies Mrs. Ramsay and undertakes her artistic project. What begins as detached observation teases toward "intimacy," which tests Lily's objectivity and risks the authenticity of her representation: "What art was there … by which one pressed through into those secret chambers? What device for becoming, like waters poured into one jar, inextricably the same, one with the object one adored?" (51). Though Lily wants "unity" with Mrs. Ramsay, "Nothing happened"; Mrs. Ramsay remains isolated, the "shape of a dome." This fact motivates Lily to try and "connect this mass on the right hand with that on the left" through art (53). Woolf's examination of accumulation's potential to dissolve is not without misgivings. Lily has doubts about the changes that must take place, and she fears that the "unity of the whole might be broken." Mrs. Ramsay resists accumulation, while Lily investigates its liberating potential. The Ramsay matriarch ostensibly desires unification, but her utmost desire is to cast a "dome" around her children, to protect them from the destruction outside.

With the additional layer of time, the deteriorating summer home in the novel's middle section, "Time Passes," exemplifies entropy not as state, but as process. Entropy and time are linked: the "irreversibility of heat transfer," typified in the entropic process, is the "archetypal physical manifestation of temporal irreversibility" (Lestienne 114). "Time Passes" features emotional human experiences that parallel the decay of the summer home, suggesting profound links between time and accumulation. As Fraser puts it, "Woolf depicts the collapse of the house ... as a trajectory of decay that ... resonates with the other instances of artistic creation that bracket it in the first and third parts of the novel. Art in *To the Lighthouse* is less about the art work than art working" (128). Woolf's portrayal of Mrs. Ramsay "working"—her efforts to keep things different, separate—confirms her keen insight into the effects of accumulation on both small and large scales. Woolf concludes that complete freedom from time or entropy is unrealistic.

We see time embodied in daughter Cam Ramsay, who "would not stop" and subsequently makes it to the Lighthouse (Woolf 54). Conversely, Mrs. Ramsay wants to stop time, "her old antagonist" (79). She feels "ashamed of her own shabbiness" as time passes (57). She "never wanted James to grow a day older! or Cam either" (58). Her husband, on the other hand, embraces the passage of time, calling his wife's desire to freeze it a "gloomy view of life" (59). Indeed, Mrs. Ramsay is at odds with not only time and entropic decay, but life itself. She removes herself from life, attempts to close herself off, as a battle unfolds: "A sort of transaction went on between them, in which she was on one side, and life was on another, and she was always trying to get the better of it, as it was of her" (59).

That Mrs. Ramsay will fall in battle has already been made clear in the novel's well-known dinner scene, the climax of the first section, "The Window." What should be a representation of victory over time and chaos is instead a picture of Mrs. Ramsay's loosening grasp on order. She opines, "nothing seemed to have merged. They all sat separate. And the whole of the effort of merging and flowing and creating rested on her" (83). In this moment, Mrs. Ramsay allies with time, "giving herself the little shake that one gives a watch that has stopped, the old familiar pulse ... beating, as the watch begins ticking." She yields to the flow of time, allowing for an emotional release in the form of "pity" for William Bankes (84). Lily "watched her drifting into that strange no-man's land where to follow people is impossible and yet their going inflicts such a chill on those who watch them that they always try." Mrs. Ramsay acquiesces, weathering a chill as heat is drawn from the room.

Mrs. Ramsay predicts her own collapse, meanwhile locating hope for future stability in the union of family friends Paul Rayley and Minta Doyle:

> 'the Rayleys'—she tried the new name over; and she felt ... that community of feeling with other people which emotions gives as if the walls of partition had become so thin that practically (the feeling was one of relief and happiness) it was all one stream, and chairs, tables, maps, were hers, were theirs, it did not matter whose, and [they] would carry it on when she was dead. (113–14)

She is energized by this image, two becoming one, but she fails to achieve the same sense of community in her own marriage. Her assent to time and accumulation allows for merging of a kind, when she puts herself in Minta's place, "like a girl of twenty" when "drawing Minta's wrap round her" (116–17).

The partition around Mrs. Ramsay is at its thinnest in the final pages of "The Window," as a cross-contamination occurs between her and her husband: "something seemed ... to go from him to her" (119). This exchange of "life" affects her such that her husband no longer gives a "damn who reached Z" (119–20). Solely focused on his wife, he "forgot himself completely," yet his domineering nature remains (120). As he "exaggerated her ignorance, her simplicity" in his assessment, "Her beauty seemed ... to increase" (121). In his observation of his wife's waning influence, she becomes altogether more satisfying. He threatens total absorption of her, "to close round her" (122). Mrs. Ramsay's final resistance punctuates this near merging, for even though she is eclipsed by her husband's chaos, she denies her husband the "sympathy" he craves, opting for the symbol of a more distant concern, the "stocking" she creates for the boy in the Lighthouse.

Mrs. Ramsay's death in "Time Passes" ushers in a comprehensive merging where "all ceased together, gathered together" (127). Without her resistance, we witness an overall decline of useful work within the system, shown in the "light which mellows the energy of labour" (127). As entropy builds toward a maximum, new opportunities for empathy emerge. Marco Caracciolo points out that the "deep significance of this section lies in the challenge it poses to the reader: it constructs a fictional world literally perceived by no one; but in doing so it foregrounds the absence of this perceiving consciousness, so that readers are themselves forced to enter the world projected by the text and occupy its central blank" (262). Woolf draws the arrow of time as if it were "woven around the invisible body of the reader," implicating us in the process of creation in this grand empathic gesture (Caracciolo 281).

When Lily returns to the house in the novel's final section, "The Lighthouse," she feels the absence of Mrs. Ramsay, "as if the link that usually bound things together had been cut" (Woolf 146). But despite how "chaotic" things appear to her now, the survivors congregate nonetheless on a "beautiful still day" (146). Lily remains the keenest observer, maintaining distance within her own subsystem quite successfully, what she thinks of as sidestepping "Human relations" (92). As Mrs. Ramsay resists entropy and time, Lily resists accumulation in the form of these relations: "she need not marry, thank Heaven: she need not undergo that degradation. She was saved from that dilution" (102). Though distanced from others, Lily feels that same tearing apart, the flux that Mrs. Ramsay endures. She was "made to feel violently two opposite things at the same time" (102). Her affinity for Mrs. Ramsay inspires her to take up her failed mission, to re-erect the "barrier" in order "to ward off Mr. Ramsay" (149). But she, too, will fail to stay the necessary accumulation of entropy Mr. Ramsay heralds. For we know that her barrier, her painting, will only add to the accumulation of waste, "rolled up and stuffed under a sofa" (158).

Woolf reveals Mr. Ramsay's unchecked dominion by virtue of his redoubled influence over Cam and James, "acquiescent in their father's wake" (155). So encompassed, they cross over the "edge of the lawn," united in a "common feeling." These three are now "bound together," and they enter the "final phase," crossing over into "some other region" (156). Cam and James are further united by their matrilineal resistance of their father, their "great compact—to resist tyranny to the death" (163). Interpersonal merging intensifies on the boat, not just between the Ramsays, but also with Mr. Macalister and his son, to the degree that Mr. Ramsay sounds different: a "little tinge of Scottish accent … came into his voice, making him seem like a peasant himself" (164). Cam becomes defamiliarized with her previous surroundings; as they sail further and further from the house into this "other region," the shore they left behind looks like "something receding in which one has no longer any part" (166). The order of the past becomes obsolete: the "sea was more important now than the shore" (191). Even Lily seeks out the symbol of chaos: "And Mr. Ramsay? She wanted him" (202).

As disorder spreads, people die, marriages fall apart, and yet all the degradation in *To the Lighthouse* leads to equilibrium. Woolf writes *To the Lighthouse* in the "vocabulary of chaos," and this is not a wholly negative truth (McFarlane 92). The "defining thing in the Modernist mode is not so much that things fall *apart* but that they fall *together* … . In Modernism, the center is seen exerting not a centrifugal but a centripetal force; and the consequence is not disintegration but (as it were) superintegration" ([italics original] McFarlane 92). Lily's final brushstroke represents the centripetal force that enables superintegration, and the remarkable interpersonal connections in the latter pages of Woolf's novel anticipate the end of the accumulative process. For instance, exchanges of thought suggesting something as extreme as telepathy occur between Lily and Mr. Carmichael: they "had not needed to speak. They had been thinking the same things and he had answered her without her asking him anything" (Woolf 208). James identifies with the Sorleys in the Lighthouse to the degree that it "confirmed some obscure feeling of his about his own self character" (203). This interpersonal merging is punctuated by a final symbolic addition to the buildup of waste in the system. Mr. Ramsay "sprinkled the crumbs from his sandwich paper" in the sea, proceeding to step outside himself, crossing the barrier separating him from James and providing his son the "praise" he had so long withheld (206). Something of James is reflected in his father, as he "sprang, lightly like a young man" (207). When Mr. Ramsay completes his wife's commitment, finally delivering the goods to the "Lighthouse men," what we realize is that James and his father *are* these men, the barriers between people that Mrs. Ramsay found "Insoluble" now dissolved (207). Though Mr. Ramsay fails to make it to "Z," he completes the quest his wife could not; and even though his wife's solitary energies were insufficient, her absence is the catalyst for the combined efforts of her husband and Lily. As stated above, Lily repurposes the chaos in Mr. Ramsay's wake such that useful renovation manifests. Indeed, Lily's mission is of "one and the same effort," as she concedes that her painting will "be destroyed. But what did that matter?" (208). Lily's "laying down her brush in extreme fatigue" signals that equilibrium has been reached. Ultimately, Woolf provides a case study of the necessity of unification, the advantages of accumulation, the potential of combined effort to "lump all the letters together in one flash—the way of genius" (34).

Works Cited

Brown, Paul Tolliver. "Relativity, Quantum Physics, and Consciousness in Virginia Woolf's To the Lighthouse." *Journal of Modern Literature*, vol. 32, no. 3, 2009, pp. 39–62. *EBSCOhost*, https://doi.org/10.2979/JML.2009.32.3.39.

Caracciolo, Marco. "Leaping into Space: The Two Aesthetics of *To the Lighthouse*." *Poetics Today*, vol. 31, no. 2, 2010, pp. 251–284. *EBSCOhost*, https://doi.org/10.1215/03335372-2009-020.

Cuda, Anthony. *The Passions of Modernism: Eliot, Yeasts, Woolf, and Mann*. University of South Carolina Press, 2010.

Frank, Adam J. and Elizabeth A. Wilson. *A Silvan Tomkins Handbook: Foundations for Affect Theory*. University of Minnesota Press, 2020. *Project MUSE* muse.jhu.edu/book/78624.

Fraser, Graham. "The Fall of the House of Ramsay: Virginia Woolf's Ahuman Aesthetics of Ruin." *Criticism: A Quarterly for Literature and the Arts*, vol. 62, no. 1, 2020, pp. 117–141. EBSCOhost, http://search.ebscohost.com/login.aspx?direct=true&db=mzh&AN=202019534468&site=ehost-live.

Gilman, Benjamin Ives. "Art a Tryst." *The Arts*, vol. 6, no. 1, 1924.

Hatfield, Elaine, et al. "Emotional Contagion." *Current Directions in Psychological Science*, vol. 2, no. 3, 1993, pp. 96–99. *JSTOR*, www.jstor.org/stable/20182211. Accessed 9 Oct. 2020.

Lakoff, George and Mark Johnson. *Metaphors We Live By*. The University of Chicago Press, 1980.

Lestienne, Remy. *The Children of Time: Causality, Entropy, Becoming*. Translated by E. C. Neher. University of Illinois Press, 1995.

McFarlane, James. "The Mind of Modernism." *Modernism: A Guide to European Literature 1890–1930*, edited by Malcolm Bradbury and James McFarlane, Penguin, 1991, pp. 71–93.

Miller, J. Hillis. "Mr. Carmichael and Lily Briscoe: The Rhythm of Creativity in *To the Lighthouse*." *Modernism Reconsidered*, edited by Robert Kiely and John Hildebidle, Harvard University Press, 1983, pp. 167–89.

Sausman, Justin. "From Vibratory Occultism to Vibratory Modernism: Blackwood, Lawrence, Woolf." *Vibratory Modernism*, edited by Anthony Enns and Shelley Trower, Palgrave Macmillan, 2013, pp. 30–52.

Woolf, Virginia. *To the Lighthouse*. Houghton Mifflin Harcourt, 1989.

CHAPTER 5

Darkening Empathy in Eugene O'Neill's *Long Day's Journey into Night*

Abstract Eugene O'Neill presents a quasi-biographical family drama in his best-known play, *Long Day's Journey into Night*. O'Neill's tragedy reveals a once-thriving family unit breaking down around matriarch Mary, who reveals that the play's only means of escape is a total splitting of the self. One Mary, as it were, embraces entropy, and as the curtain descends, she is changed, while the men around her stagnate. If entropy and time go hand in hand, the final scene of *Long Day's Journey* shows that Mary captures something of a long-lost past, a snapshot of a happier time, before James and his stultifying influence inculcated her in a pattern of degradation, self-loathing, and endless pursuit. Still, a darkening dominates the play, such that the Tyrones live out their days in a monotonous loop, clouded by past tragedy.

Keywords Anger · Black Humor · Disorder · Equilibrium · Empathy · Entropy · Heat death · Humiliation · *Long Day's Journey into Night* · O'Neill, Eugene · Shame

"We are such stuff as manure is made on," ironically replies Edmund Tyrone, as his father chides him for forgetting his Shakespeare (O'Neill 796). In Eugene O'Neill's *Long Day's Journey into Night*, Patriarch James Tyrone clings to the words of the bard, assuring his youngest that he will find all that is "worth saying" therein. Edmund, however, is more interested in the decadents, "third-raters" to James, suggesting that his artistic tastes are far and away from whatever timeless wisdom Shakespeare bestowed. *Long Day's Journey*, O'Neill's best-known play, is full of such exchanges, a fact that highlights the diminishing returns characteristic of the Tyrone family. James's waning "vitality" is duplicated in firstborn Jamie's "premature disintegration" and "dissipation" (722). Matriarch Mary's "girlishness" likewise dwindles, suggesting images of some "ghost of the dead" (728). No Tyrone wants to accept responsibility for the family's bleak predicament. Mary, for example, blames Edmund for the decay, noting that her hair "began to turn white" following his birth (728). Not to mention that the whole affair plays out under the shadow of the heartbreaking infant death of son Eugene. O'Neill's tragedy reveals a once-thriving unit breaking down, together with any symbolic weight notions of family and community convey.

Moving away from more expressionist and symbolic plays and toward tragic realism in the late 1930s and early 1940s, O'Neill composed *The Iceman Cometh* and *Long Day's Journey into Night*. Posthumously published in 1956, *Long Day's Journey* depicts the plight of the Tyrone family, who are dealing with the combined misery of a morphine-addicted, suicidal matriarch and the worsening health of youngest Edmund due to tuberculosis. Washed-up play actor James and idle oldest son Jamie round out the family. As the Tyrones live out their days in their country home drinking and arguing, an encroaching fog closes in, sealing them off from the outside world. In time, Mary relapses into addiction and Edmund's health worsens, and the Tyrones's world degenerates into seemingly inescapable entropic collapse.

The Tyrones's system is perilously close to exhaustion. Their actions—or lack thereof add to ever-accumulating waste. Hard-working Tyrone is succeeded by Jamie, a "lazy lunk and sponge" (731). Jamie's influence spreads to his younger brother Edmund, who is "poisoned" and "old before his time" (732). This deterioration is accompanied by a pattern of iteration: past events repeat in the present, accumulating into what we might call a strong theory. For example, James's father is rumored to have committed suicide: "He mistook rat poison for flour, or sugar, or something. There was gossip it wasn't by mistake" (807). Edmund likewise attempts suicide, as does Mary. Mary's father dies from consumption, the same disease that presently afflicts Edmund. The Tyrone men persistently resist the shame they feel for Mary, such that in time shame becomes humiliation. Repeated ad nauseum, these actions lead to anger, fuel for the affects. This pattern forecasts further amplification of shame, further conversion of shame into humiliation, further anger at the feelings of humiliation. What comes into view is a degenerating system that encourages its inhabitants to escape, to seek survival elsewhere. For if one fails to escape, they are destined for stagnation: "I'd lost the great talent I once had through years of easy repetition," James says, "never learning a new part, never really working hard"; we see him "ossified" before the play's end (809, 814).

O'Neill portrays in striking detail the undoing of a family and the far-reaching implications consequent to its collapse. Daniel Larner argues that "we live in a world, as O'Neill paints it, which is itself exhausted, which has had its meaning eaten away by an eagle no one remembers, as punishment for a crime long since dissipated in oceans of time. We are caught by our own longings in an endless Promethean ritual, which we are doomed to repeat" (10). How can the Tyrones thrive when their world is equally disintegrated? This air of hopelessness seems fitting for the play, which is often remembered for its tragic features. But by this late stage in O'Neill's career, "tragedy has … become only an echo of a tragic cataclysm that occurred long ago—so long ago that we can remember neither its events nor its meaning" (Larner 10). *Long Day's Journey* occurs in aftermath, well-removed from the impetus of any remarkable disaster. In this way, the unpleasant details of the play are dulled, reiterated in the players' consistent efforts to deaden themselves with drink, drugs, and self-harm.

These entropic conditions increase empathic potential. However, a darkening dominates the play, such that there is no substantial benefit in equilibrium. The Tyrones live out their days in a monotonous loop, clouded by past tragedy. Their actions, carried out for ostensibly their own sake, without hope of change, run together until the Tyrones forget why it is they behave this way. Case in point, the men take great pains to hide Edmund's worsening illness from Mary, but she has already relapsed into addiction. Such truths, though not hysterically comic, do approach the appreciably absurd. The at times good-humored Tyrones know this and are "dully resigned" to the fact: they've "lived with this before and … must again. There's no help for it" (E759). And as the play unfolds, the dower tone becomes increasingly interspersed with moments of laughter, to the extent that Jamie calls it all a "game" (818).

O'Neill presents a complicated picture of the humorous in *Long Day's Journey*. To be sure, one's worldview largely dictates one's appreciation of humor. Patrick O'Neill, tracing evolving theories of comedy and tragedy from Friedrich Nietzsche's in the nineteenth century to Mikhail Bakhtin's in the next, surmises that the "distinction between tragedy and comedy" became "increasingly blurred during the twentieth century" (55–58). What emerged was "entropic" humor, or humor "influenced precisely by entropic modes of thought" (24). Entropic humor is in some ways like black humor: comedy that "presents tragic, distressing, or morbid situations in humorous terms" ("black humor"). Non-entropic humor, so to speak, often relies on chaotic situations or misunderstandings; these situations tend to make us laugh because they tease the limits of our daily experience of an ostensibly orderly world (P. O'Neill 50). So-called normative, humor depends on "contrast—and contrast is always associated with an implicit or explicit notion of order" (47, 46). Repetition to the point of absurdity, laughter during disaster, all symptoms of Eugene O'Neill's worldview, what he calls a "gorgeously-ironical, beautifully-indifferent, splendidly-suffering bit of chaos" (qtd. in Dowling 10). Under the "entropic" humor umbrella is "entropic satire" (P. O'Neill 201). Entropic satire is different from the other types of satire in terms of its "moral efficacy":

> At the more benign end of its spectrum satire is characterized by a firm belief in its own moral efficacy, by a confidence that what is broken can be mended … . As this confidence wanes, … so satire slides over into its entropic mode, where disorder is acknowledged as triumphing over order, and didactic confidence gives way to a fascinated vision of maximum entropy, total disorder. (133)

Long Day's Journey works as entropic satire because it "remain[s] entirely unchanged, totally impassive to any impact, ameliorative or otherwise, on the part of the characters" (201). O'Neill's satirical portrait of a family in aftermath suggests no remedy, instead flaunting the Tyrone's sole outcome.

Characters in entropic systems often self-isolate, a metaphorical move especially relevant to modernism: the "modernist relativized the everyday world by projecting alternative, fictional worlds where different norms obtained—where a man might wake up one morning, for example, and find himself, like Kafka's Gregor Samsa, metamorphosed into a monstrous insect" (P. O'Neill 61); the "archetypal realist text … admits of no distance and no difference between itself and the reality it reproduces; the modernist text is a product precisely of this distance and difference" (62). *Long Day's Journey* is about distance: even as the Tyrones fall into each other—physically, emotionally—the result is a family that could not be further apart. "O'Neill succeeds in … creating a powerful allegorical ordering of family as community," writes Michael Brandon Lopez, "and in this case a lost community that is so close, and yet as the day progresses into night and day once again, finds itself ever farther away from each member" (73–74). This is appropriate for a play that bookends modernism. Set near the beginning of the era and composed near its end, the Tyrones are a modern family that, in attempting to fall back on the wisdom and order of the past, are smothered under the chaotic and undeniable realities of the present.

In isolation, characters frequently experience a heightened capacity for empathy and the novel ability to "bypass or neutralize" what Fritz Breithaupt calls "empathy-blocking mechanisms" (83). To adapt Breithaupt, entropy is a "catalyst" for empathic events (89). Partitions become traversable under appropriate conditions: "Blocking mechanisms may also be circumvented via a temporary allowance of empathy … . We might imagine this as a kind of pulse, whereby the barrier becomes passable for a short period of time then closes again. Certain moods, for example, stimulate us to 'lower the gate' for a while" (92). Mary's relapse gives the Tyrone men a common concern. Edmund's waning health pulls some attention away from her, but Mary's health is priority. For example, the men collude to hide the truth of Edmund's degrading health from her. Altogether, she tends to bind the family. The focus on Mary generates a common bond between her husband and eldest son: "*His son looks at him, for the first time with an understanding sympathy. It is as if suddenly a deep bond of common feeling existed between them in which their antagonisms could be forgotten*" (734).[1] Mary is the transformative referent of the men's emotions, which creates an empathic space for them to share. She is also a "ghost of the dead" who degrades physically and mentally before the men's eyes. Lopez argues that "none of the Tyrones can forsake individual pain rooted deeply within the inability to acknowledge fully the debt to one another in love, and consequently each member lapses into a destructive submersion of independent miseries and sorrows" (74). The empathic bonds the Tyrones share are fleeting—pulses—and ultimately insufficient to provide rescue. O'Neill shows this through Mary's "atmosphere of

---

[1] These and all italics hereafter original.

constant suspicion": "If there was only some place I could go to get away" (E. O'Neill 740). In a sense, an entropic satire of the very notion of genuine empathy. "It would be better were this community destroyed," argues Lopez, "its members set free from one another … in order to discover their own selves within, and ultimately to recognize their debt of love to each other" (74).

But the Tyrones only draw closer together. O'Neill's controlling metaphor, the image of ever-encroaching fog that surrounds and cuts off the family from the outside world communicates this well. Encased in fog, the Tyrones become more introverted as time passes. For instance, James's chaotic potential to loses its edge; and even when he speaks to his sons "caustically," he is met with a discourteous offer, delivered "dully" (O'Neill 751). Mary blames the passage of time for the state of the family, proclaiming to Edmund that Jamie "can't help being what the past has made him. Any more than your father can. Or you. Or I." The past casts an overbearing authority over the present, and it holds a stultifying power over all the play's possible futures: "all significant action has taken place in the past," as Doris Falk puts it; "the present consequence is despair" (199). Appropriate, considering the "progress of O'Neill's mind," which "was steadily away from an outer world where purposeful activity or event … were important, through an inner world where conflict is important, to an innermost world where nothing is important" (Falk 199). O'Neill's personal development—a transition of the mind through various "worlds"—is one possible reason why *Long Day's Journey* presents such a dark vision of empathy. "The past is the present, isn't it? It's the future, too" (O'Neill 765).

Long Day's Journey is an autobiographical play about a "hated self" (Falk 199). As the family inverts, they are forced to face that self. The empathy they experience is based on an experience of the self, tainted with hate. Self-loathing spreads, infecting the family's view of each other. Mary simultaneously and equally blames herself and Jamie for baby Eugene's death: "I've always believed Jamie did it on purpose. He was jealous of the baby. He hated him," she laments (O'Neill 765). Breithaupt questions "whether increased empathy is an unalloyed good thing" (67). As he puts it:

> empathy entails the risk of self-loss as an effect of taking on the perspective of another, leading to a weakening of one's own interests, feelings, self-perception, intensity, identity, self-esteem, or self-awareness. This does not

mean losing a basic and existing psychological faculty like the ego (as imagined by Freud) but rather bestowing a self onto the other, conceived of (by Nietzsche and others) as overly powerful, more real, and more important than the idea one has of oneself. This bestowal has the effect of hollowing or thinning out the idea of one's own self. Perhaps instead of self-loss, it would be more appropriate to speak of self-production, but of a self that is denied to the observer and attributed only to the observed other. (81)

If this dark version of empathy is what we see in *Long Day's Journey*, what we are ultimately witnessing is a widespread "hollowing," an empathic emptying out of all the players, a fading of the self in exchange for a new observed other. In this entropic satiric, all are doomed to repetition and diminishment. It may very well be that the Tyrones, in the perpetual shadow of past tragedy, despairingly seek to empathize with baby Eugene, the one who is lost and cannot be communed with:

> the empathetic observer lives in pursuit of others. They experience and feel what the others might. This is the literal meaning of resentment: re-sentiment, a secondhand feeling, the condition of being always in pursuit. The empathetic person has no feelings of their own, at least not strong ones full of passion. Instead, they relive the feelings of others. In this sense, as Nietzsche sees it [in *On the Genealogy of Morals*], empathy is, structurally, resentment. (Breithaupt 55)

This is a treacherous situation. As everything breaks down around the Tyrones, unfulfilled desires to bond foment a growing sense of antipathy. James speaks with "guilty resentment" when he rebukes Mary for dwelling on the past; Mary in turn only further removes herself by entering deeper into the past (O'Neill 765). "For God's sake," says James, "don't dig up what's long forgotten. If you're that far gone in the past already, when it's only the beginning of the afternoon, what will you be tonight?" Despite Mary's clear desire to escape, she exists in a state of flux: "She'll listen but she won't listen. She'll be here but she won't be here" (760). As she states, "bearing Edmund was the last straw" (765). Mary passes the point of no return: the accumulation of entropy in the system has reached a breaking point.

As day transforms into night, O'Neill shows Mary march further and further into "*strange detachment*" (772). Her physical appearance mirrors this change: she becomes "*paler… and her eyes shine with unnatural brilliance.*" She comes to embrace isolation: "I really love fog," she says. "It hides you from the world and the world from you. You feel that everything has changed, and nothing is what it seemed to be. No one can find or touch you any more" (773). Mary's acquiescence is reflected in outward signs of disorder: the "careless, almost slovenly way" she dresses; the fact that her "*hair is no longer fastidiously in place. It has a slightly disheveled, lopsided look*" (772).[2] Mary finds "*refuge and release in a dream where present reality is but an appearance to be accepted and dismissed unfeelingly ... or entirely ignored*" (italics original). She likewise recounts her physical degradation: "Poor hands! You'd never believe it, but they were once one of my good points, along with my hair and eyes, and I had a fine figure, too" (776).[3]

A character's "personal entropy" has the potential to be "projected over the world around them" (Tanner 147). By extension, the emotional side effects of increased personal entropy also spread. Mary's paranoia is transferred to Edmund, who is "born afraid," as Mary was "afraid to bring [him] into the world" (O'Neill 782). When Mary undergoes an "abrupt transformation into a detached bullying motherliness," Edmund "shrinks back into himself" (788). James fails to escape because he fights against entropy, namely, heat: "There's no reason to have the house ablaze with electricity at this time of night, burning up money!" (793). James sees others as "wasteful fools." He, too, clings to the past, but he selects aspects of the past that hold long-lasting truth and value for him: for example, Shakespeare. Less interested in a past version of himself, he romanticizes a halcyon worldview he finds in Shakespeare. What's more, James rejects Edmund's interest in the decadents, whom he calls "degenerates," an appropriate fact considering his rejection of progress, even in the literary arts (799). Conversely, Edmund embraces degeneration, sensing it may provide a way out of the system. James cannot embrace this point of view, as he values too highly Shakespeare's reputation and, as a Shakespearean actor, his own. Mary is comparably nostalgic about the early days of their relationship: James "was different from all ordinary men, like someone from another world ... I fell in love right then. So did he, he told me afterwards. I forgot all about becoming a nun or a concert pianist. All I

---

[2] This transformation results in a dissolution of barriers, in this case, barriers of class. As entropy accumulates around Mary, she "*talks to Cathleen with a confiding familiarity, as if the second girl were an old, intimate friend*" (italics original, O'Neill 772).

[3] Mary's physical breakdown typifies what Zbigniew Lewicki calls a "symbolic representation" (81) of entropy, the "gradual reduction from the animate to the inanimate" (80).

wanted was to be his wife" (778). She finds James's difference appealing, believing that entrance into another world is more important than accomplishing her former life goals. Her identification with James is the impetus for the events that transpire for the rest of the play. James's influence on her is the impetus for the hopeless cycle in which the Tyrones find themselves.

The more naturalistic moments of the play show Mary behaving like an "automaton" (789) and James acting "mechanically" (786). In fact, Mary admits her loss of control: "I hope, sometime, without meaning it, I will take an overdose. I never could do it deliberately. The Blessed Virgin would never forgive me, then" (789). Mary wants to escape the system, but she is unwilling go against her, albeit diminished, faith. Mary is at a point where the best remedy in her mind is total obliteration: "I should never have borne [Edmund]," she says (790). "It would have been better for his sake. I could never hurt him then." Conversely, James discourages abandoning the system. For one, he locks away the liquor to keep it from Jamie, who would use it as a means of temporary escape. James reassures Mary that their plight is no fault of their own, a result of a "curse put on [her] without [her] knowing or willing it." James won't accept that escape is the only way forward. Edmund presses him: "facts don't mean a thing, do they? What you want to believe, that's the only truth!" (793). Ever taking after Mary, Edmund "love[s] the fog" (795). He longs to be a specter, just like Mary, the "mad ghost" (790):

> That's what I wanted—to be alone with myself in another world where truth is untrue and life can hide from itself. Out beyond the harbor, ... I even lost the feeling of being on land. The fog and the sea seemed part of each other. ... As if I had drowned long ago. As if I was a ghost belonging to the fog, and the fog was the ghost of the sea. It felt damned peaceful to be nothing more than a ghost within a ghost. (796)

Edmund's joyous walk through the fog reminded him of the sea, fitting since the "high spots" of his life are "all connected with the sea" (811). When Edmund discusses the sea, he speaks of a great equilibrium akin to heat death: "I became drunk with the beauty and singing rhythm of [the sea], and for a moment I lost myself—actually lost my life. I was set free! I dissolved in the sea, became white sails and flying spray, became beauty and rhythm, became moonlight and the ship and the high dimmed-starred sky!" (812). He describes other times when he "Became the sun, the hot sand, green seaweed anchored to a rock, swaying in the tide. ... Like the veil of things as they seem drawn back by an unseen hand. For a second you see—and seeing the secret, are the secret. For a second there is meaning!" Granted these reveries are lofty and obscure. Even Edmund is uncertain as to what he experiences: "I belonged ... within something greater than my own life, or the life of Man, to Life itself! To God, if you want to put it that way." He gestures toward some indeterminate concept of a higher power. Laurin Porter notes that it is the "vicious cycle of family disintegration that drives [Edmund] out onto the beach in the first place" (85). She argues that each of the Tyrones lives in continual pursuit of "ideal moments, in which opposites were cancelled out and everything seemed possible" (84). All but Edmund's "moments" harbor a "familial component" (85). For him, however, the "transcendence" he experienced was out at sea, away from everyone, and his hopes to recreate them rely on a "merging with the elements" (Porter 85). What Edmund experiences is a result of "hyperempathy":

> Both biology and culture lead us towards empathy. Our social environment effectively cultivates empathy because our emotional and intellectual understanding of others gives us palpable advantages. We are incited, trained, and seduced by empathy. We also live in a world of empathetic noise. Not only other people but also various media compete for our emotional attention, further exciting our tendency towards empathetic identification. In brief, we are hyperempathetic beings. (Breithaupt 80–81)

Edmund is motivated into these empathic experiences by his biological makeup. In this sense, empathy is a natural process, like entropy. In *Long Day's Journey*, the entropic process is in its late stages, meaning that the pathways to empathic experiences are well-worn. Despite this, James stalwartly denies his wife's need for escape: "She was never made to renounce the world" (O'Neill 801). But Edmund, more attuned to his mother's needs, acknowledges the "blank wall she builds around her," likening it to a "bank of fog in which she hides and loses herself." Jamie's dejectedness reveals a pattern: "this time Mama had me fooled," he says (818). It is remarkable that Mary's pattern of addiction and deception—her practised act of escape—makes way for a display of sincere emotion from Jamie, whose subsequent "*weeping ... appears sober, not the maudlin tears of drunkenness.*" This emotional display kindles a moment of deep connection with Edmund: "I love your guts," says Jamie; "I know that," Edmund replies. Through iteration, the Tyrones tease escape. "[B]ecause I once wanted to write," Jamie tells Edmund, "I planted it in your mind that someday you'd write! Hell, you're more than my brother. I made you! You're my Frankenstein!" (819). Edmund, the younger, the newer version of Jamie, may get them closer to their goal. Indeed, iteration—which is to say, accumulation—provides hope for the Tyrones. Porter argues the following:

> Edmund's ideal moments can be repeated. Unlike the ideals of the other Tyrones, which are experienced at a specific point in the past and are therefore irretrievable, Edmund's transcendent moments seem to hold out hope for the future, since they are repeatable. This potential, however, is ironically mocked by Edmund's consumption, which threatens to rob him of life itself. Thus for Edmund, too, time is the enemy. (86)

Jamie's visits to the nearby brothel are another example of the complex blend of pursuit, self-loathing, and resentment that characterize the play. Joseph Cordaro has this to say about O'Neill's reference to Mary Shelley's *Frankenstein*:

> As Jamie equates female drug users with prostitutes, his presence in the brothel demonstrates that he is searching for a companion that is a reflection of his mother. In addition, Jamie's choice of Fat Violet recalls [Shelley's] daemon's wish that the female companion be an image of the self … . Essentially useless, [Violet] stays around the house and cadges on its owner. Disliked, alcoholic, and unable to support herself, Violet is Jamie's own female double, in addition to being a reflection of his mother. (122)

Jamie seeks Violet out for both "sympathy and empathy" (Cordaro 122). But as we have seen, empathy in the play is something closer to resentment. Jamie's temporary escapes to the brothel only leave him hollower. In David Palmer's words:

> Narcissism is one reason that [the Tyrones's] reconciliation fails. O'Neill's wounded-soul narcissists are people who feel betrayed by the world, which they perceive primarily as a set of means to the satisfaction of their own ends. As much as they may love other people, they tend not to fully recognize other people as equals who have their own needs and loves that deserve the same respect the narcissists want for their own … . This idea helps to explain the endless dance of blame and recrimination, despite abiding love, in *Long*

> *Day's Journey*. The Tyrones, while admitting their flaws, experience themselves more as victims than transgressors. They ask each other to forget the past, but the past cannot be forgotten until reconciliation is achieved, and reconciliation cannot be even pursued while they each demand of the others a plea for forgiveness. The Tyrones cannot find a shared story of the past that meets each individual's narcissistic need to be portrayed primarily as a victim rather than a transgressor. (145–146)

Despite the confusing transposition of the creator and the creation, O'Neill's *Frankenstein* reference suggests that Edmund is more akin to Victor Frankenstein than Jamie: "Edmund is Jamie's creator because he is responsible for one event in Jamie's life from which Jamie has never recovered: the loss of Mary to drugs" (Cordaro 123). This ability to create, even within a crumbling world, is perhaps the play's redemption. It is remarkable that the Tyrones's situations allows Edmund to take on the creator's role. His musings often recount the moments he is farthest from his family, his words creating a wall or sorts around him.

Edmund, however, is not the only Tyrone capable of creation. It is time that the Tyrones fight against most, proven in Mary's continual attempts to return to the past. By the play's close, she may succeed, but not in the way she intends. Steven F. Bloom goes as far as to say that there are actually "two Marys in the play—the Mary onstage, the recovering Mary," as well as the "Mary that the men fear she will regress to" (231). The play's only realistic means of escape, it would seem, is cleaving, total splitting of the self. One Mary, as it were, is hopelessly bound to the past, a regression which defies the progression of time. The other Mary, however, embraces entropy, as when she finally reveals herself "existing in a realm of her own making, beyond the reach of the world in which she actually lives" (Bloom 235). As the curtain descends on the Tyrones, Mary is changed, and the men "remain inert" (Bloom 237). In an act of creation like Edmund's, Mary creates a second self. This act introduces something new into the system and serves to slow the accumulation of entropy. If entropy and time go hand in hand, the final scene of *Long Day's Journey* shows that Mary captures something of a long-lost past, a snapshot of a happier Mary, before James and his stultifying influence inculcated her in a pattern of degradation, self-loathing, and endless pursuit. It is possible that some positive outcomes occur after the action of the play. Codaro suggests that since *Long Day's Journey* is "so closely tied to O'Neill's own life, one can argue that Edmund, who is O'Neill, will survive the consumption and go on to become a great writer" (127). Still, one is left feeling that there is only one possible conclusion for O'Neill's at times amusing recollection of a "*sad dream*" (828).

Works Cited

"black humor, n." *OED Online*, Oxford University Press, December 2020, www.oed.com/view/Entry/282814. Accessed 2 Dec. 2020.

Bloom, Steven F. "'The Mad Scene: Enter Ophelia!': O'Neill's Use of the Delayed Entrance in *Long Day's Journey into Night*." *The Eugene O'Neill Review*, vol. 26, 2004, pp. 226–238. EBSCO*host*, http://search.ebscohost.com/login.aspx?direct=true&db=mzh&AN=2004531762&site=ehost-live.

Breithaupt, Fritz. *The Dark Sides of Empathy*. Cornell University Press, 2019. *ProQuest Ebook Central*, http://ebookcentral.proquest.com/lib/uncg/detail.action?docID=5763923.

Cordaro, Joseph. "Long Day's Journey into *Frankenstein*." *The Eugene O'Neill Review*, vol. 18, no. 1/2, 1994, pp. 116–128. JSTOR, www.jstor.org/stable/29784529. Accessed 23 Jan. 2021.

Dowling, Robert M. *Eugene O'Neill: A Life in Four Acts*. Yale University Press, 2014. EBSCO*host*, http://search.ebscohost.com/login.aspx?direct=true&db=nlebk&AN=861324&site=ehost-live.

Falk, Doris V. *Eugene O'Neill and the Tragic Tension: an Interpretative Study of the Plays*, 2nd. ed. Gordian Press, 1982.

Hatfield, Elaine, et al. "Emotional Contagion." *Current Directions in Psychological Science*, vol. 2, no. 3, 1993, pp. 96–99. JSTOR, www.jstor.org/stable/20182211. Accessed 9 Oct. 2020.

Larner, Daniel. "O'Neill's Endings: The Tragicomedy of Distant Echoes." *The Eugene O'Neill Review*, vol. 31, 2009, pp. 8–16. EBSCOhost, http://search.ebscohost.com/login.aspx?direct=true&db=mzh&AN=2011280330&site=ehost-live.

Lopez, Michael Brandon. "Issues of Community in O'Neill's *Long Day's Journey into Night* and Kierkegaard's *Works of Love*." *The Eugene O'Neill Review*, vol. 31, 2009. EBSCOhost, http://search.ebscohost.com/login.aspx?direct=true&db=mzh&AN=2011280335&site=ehost-live.

O'Neill, Eugene. *Long Day's Journey into Night*. *Eugene O'Neill: Complete Plays, 1932–1943*. Library of America, 1988.

O'Neill, Patrick. *The Comedy of Entropy: Humour, Narrative, Reading*. University of Toronto Press, 1990.

Palmer, David. "Three Ways to Fail at Forgiveness: Beckett, Miller, and O'Neill." *The Eugene O'Neill Review*, vol. 36, no. 2, 2015, pp. 115–149. JSTOR, www.jstor.org/stable/10.5325/eugeoneirevi.36.2.0115. Accessed 2 Dec. 2021.

Porter, Laurin. *The Banished Prince: Time, Memory, and Ritual in the Late Plays of Eugene O'Neill.* UMI Research Press, 1988.

Tanner, Tony. "Everything Running Down." *City of Words: American Fiction 1950–1970.* Harper & Row, New York, 1971, pp. 141–52.

Index[1]

A
Accumulation, 2, 4–6, 8–10, 28, 36, 38, 50, 51, 53, 54, 56–60, 69, 73, 74
Affect, 2–4, 8–16, 8n2, 12n4, 13n5, 19, 20
  system, 2, 8, 12–14
  theory, 3, 9, 11
Anger, 9–11, 15, 39, 45, 65

B
Beckett, Samuel, 24
Black humor, 66
Brown, John, 36, 38–41, 44–46

C
Cane, 6, 35–37, 36n1, 44, 45
Chaos, 51, 53, 56–60, 66

Clausius, Rudolf, 4, 7
Conrad, Joseph, 24
Crane, Stephen, 23–33
Cybernetics, 8, 11, 12, 14

D
Dictionary of National Biography, 6
Disorder, 4–7, 9, 10, 25, 37, 51, 54, 60, 66, 70

E
Eliot, T. S., 7
Empathy, 25, 26, 29, 31, 40–43, 58, 63–75
Endgame, 25
Energy, 4–8, 10, 11, 28–30, 32, 35, 36, 40, 41, 45, 50–53, 55, 58, 60

[1] Note: Page numbers followed by 'n' refer to notes.

© The Author(s), under exclusive license to Springer Nature Switzerland AG 2025
M. Phillips, *Disorder, Affect, and Modernist Literature*, Palgrave Studies in Affect Theory and Literary Criticism,
https://doi.org/10.1007/978-3-031-92463-7

Entropic, 2, 4–7, 9–11, 9n3
Entropy, 2–11, 9n3, 17, 20, 25–28, 30, 32, 36–38, 45, 49–60, 66, 67, 69, 70, 70n2, 70n3, 72, 74
Equilibrium, 2, 6, 8, 9, 11, 28, 39, 42, 50, 53, 54, 60, 65, 71

F
Frank, Waldo, 36, 39, 39n3

G
Gilman, Benjamin Ives, 26, 27, 30, 52, 53
Gurney, Ivor, 24

H
Heart of Darkness, 24
Heat, 3, 4, 10, 11, 28, 30, 36, 45
Heat death, 2, 6, 9, 10, 26, 30, 37, 45, 50, 53, 56, 71
Humiliation, 65

L
Long Day's Journey into Night, 63–75

M
Modernism, 2–7, 19

O
O'Neill, Eugene, 63–75
Owen, Wilfred, 24

R
Renovation, 50, 53, 55, 56, 60

S
Sarte, Jean-Paul, 24
Sassoon, Siegfried, 24
Shame, 3, 9–13, 13n5, 14n6, 15–16, 15n7, 38, 40, 43, 46, 64, 65
    empathic shame, 15, 16
Stasis, 53
Stevens, Wallace, 24, 33
Strong theory, 50, 64

T
Thermodynamics, 2, 4, 9, 50
Tomkins, Silvan, 2, 3, 8, 8n2, 9, 9–10n3, 13n5, 14n6, 37–39, 44, 46, 50
Toomer, Jean, 6, 20, 35–46
To the Lighthouse, 5, 20, 49–60

W
Waste, 50–52, 55, 56, 59, 60, 64
Weiner, Norbert, 8, 12
Whitman, Walt, 24, 33
"Withered Skin of Berries," 35–46
Woolf, Virginia, 5, 20, 49
Work, 52–54, 57, 58, 66